FrontPage® 98

fast & easy™

How to Order:

For information on quantity discounts, contact the publisher: Prima Publishing, P.O. Box 1260BK, Rocklin, CA 95677-1260; (916) 632-4400. On your letterhead, include information concerning the intended use of the books and the number of books you wish to purchase. For individual orders, turn to the back of this book for more information.

FrontPage® 98

═══fast & easy™

Coletta Witherspoon

PRIMA PUBLISHING

Prima Publishing and colophon are registered trademarks of Prima Communications, Inc.
Fast & Easy is a trademark of Prima Communications, Inc. Prima Publishing, Rocklin, California 95677.

Publisher: Matthew H. Carleson
Managing Editor: Dan J. Foster
Acquisitions Editor: Jenny L. Watson
Project Editor: Kevin W. Ferns
Copy Editor: Judy A. Ohm
Technical Reviewers: Kevin W. Ferns and Ray Link
Interior Layout: Shawn Morningstar
Cover Design: Prima Design Team
Indexer: Katherine Stimson

Important: If you have problems installing or running Microsoft FrontPage 98, notify Microsoft at (425) 635-7056 or on the Web at www.microsoft.com. Prima Publishing cannot provide software support.

ISBN: 0-7615-1534-8
Library of Congress Catalog Card Number: 98-65162
Printed in the United States of America

99 00 01 HH 10 9 8 7 6 5 4 3 2

To my brother, Marcel

Acknowledgments

It takes several people, a lot of hard work, and a great deal of support to create a book.

I would like to say mahalo nui loa to Matt and Mary Lovein and the Holualoa Gallery for sharing their aloha. Matt and Mary not only graciously allowed me to use their art to make my Web pages look good, but they also gave me access to their computer equipment when mine broke. Without their help and support, I wouldn't have been able to finish this book. An extra thanks goes to Mary for being such a great e-mail buddy and for all the humorous e-mail attachments that helped alleviate some of my creativity blocks.

My never-ending thanks and love to my husband Craig, who is always my biggest supporter. Without Craig's encouragement, support, and teaching, I wouldn't be the writer that I am today.

And, of course, my thanks to everyone at Prima Publishing who helped make this book a reality. A special round of applause goes to Kevin Ferns, my faithful editor, for going the extra mile on this book and for volunteering to put on an extra hat or two when the going got rough. I would also like to thank Jenny Watson for giving me this opportunity and Judy Ohm for doing a perfect job of copy editing. You've been a great bunch of folks to work with.

About the Author

Coletta Witherspoon is a freelance writer and editor who has worked on more than a dozen computer books, most recently Prima Publishing's *Internet Explorer 4.0 Fast & Easy*. She also writes and produces marketing literature, training programs, and video scripts for corporate clients. Coletta lives in Hawaii and conducts all of her business (and much of her personal life) over the Internet.

Contents at a Glance

Contents

PART II
EXPANDING YOUR WEB 61

PART III
ENHANCING YOUR WEB 121

APPENDIX. 285

Introduction

This *Fast & Easy* guide from Prima Publishing will help you master FrontPage 98 so that you can create eye-catching Web sites. Every step in the book is accompanied by an illustration of what you will see on your computer screen, so you can easily follow along and check your results.

FrontPage is a versatile and creative Web site design and management program. FrontPage will make it easy to add the extra bells and whistles to your Web site with the help of wizards, and it contains many other tools to help you create sophisticated Web sites. Whether you have an existing Web site that you want to improve or you are designing your first Web page, you will find the information you need in this book.

WHO SHOULD READ THIS BOOK?

This book is directed toward the novice computer user that needs a hands-on approach. The generous use of illustrations makes this an ideal tool for those who have never used a Web site design program before. This book is also for those who are familiar with other Web site design programs and want to quickly apply their skills to FrontPage 98.

This book is organized so you can quickly look up tasks to help you complete a job or learn a new trick. You may need to read an entire chapter to master a subject, or you may only need to read a certain section of a chapter to refresh your memory.

SPECIAL FEATURES OF THIS BOOK

You will find other features in this book that provide more information on how to work with FrontPage 98:

✦ **Tips** offer helpful hints about features in FrontPage that make your job a little easier and add spice to your Web pages.

✦ **Notes** offer additional information about FrontPage design and use to enhance your learning experience with the new software.

Also, the appendix shows how to create a theme that you can use when building FrontPage webs. Happy designing!

PART I

Creating
Your Web

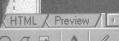

1

Getting Started with FrontPage 98

If you've never used FrontPage before, you may not know where to start. The program's unique interface and assortment of buttons and menus may overwhelm you. If you have used FrontPage before, you may need some help getting accustomed to the program's new features. But don't fret! Even though FrontPage 98 is a powerful and sophisticated program that can create complex Web sites, it's also easy to use. You'll create the foundation for your first Web site in a short time. In this chapter, you'll learn how to:

✦ Start FrontPage

✦ Move around the FrontPage Explorer

✦ Use toolbars and menus in the FrontPage Editor

✦ Get help

✦ Exit FrontPage

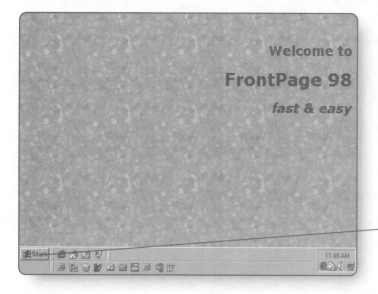

STARTING FRONTPAGE 98

Before you can begin creating your Web site, you must first open the FrontPage 98 program. It takes only a few simple mouse clicks to set you on your way.

1. **Click** on the **Start button** on the Windows Taskbar. The Start menu will appear.

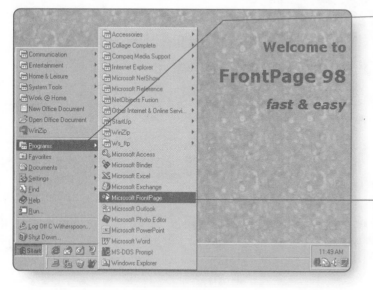

2. **Move** the **mouse pointer** to Programs. The Programs menu will appear.

3. **Click** on **Microsoft FrontPage**. FrontPage will open and the Getting Started dialog box will appear.

OPENING A WEB

After FrontPage appears on your screen, you'll need to provide a few instructions on how you want to proceed. The easiest way to start is to use one of the pre-designed templates provided with the program. The simplest template is the Personal Web. This template creates a basic web for you.

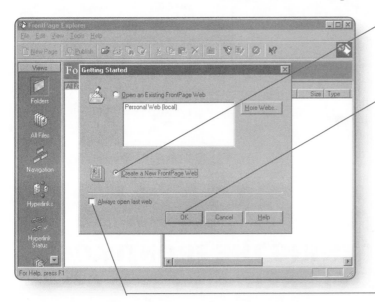

1. **Click** on the **Create a New FrontPage Web option button**. The option will be selected.

2. **Click** on **OK**. The New FrontPage Web dialog box will appear. This dialog box allows you to select the type of web to create.

TIP

You can save yourself a few mouse clicks the next time you open your FrontPage web. To automatically open the last web that you worked on, click on Always open last web.

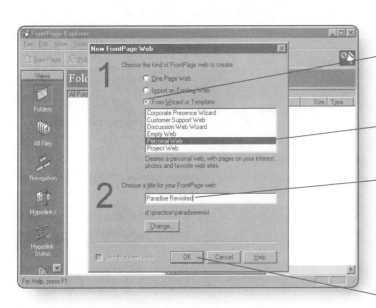

1. **Click** on the **From Wizard or Template option button**. The option will be selected.

2. **Click** on **Personal Web**. It will be selected.

3. **Type** a **title** for your web in the Choose a title for your FrontPage web: text box. This title should describe what your web is all about.

4. **Click** on **OK**.

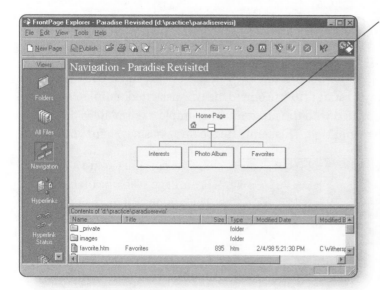

Your web will appear in the FrontPage Explorer window.

NOTE

Some of the templates provided by FrontPage use a wizard that walks you through the process of gathering content for your web. You'll learn more about wizards as you progress through this book.

VIEWING THE FRONTPAGE EXPLORER

The FrontPage Explorer helps you create and manage your FrontPage web. With FrontPage Explorer, you can organize your web's structure, move files and folders, add and delete pages and files, test hyperlinks to determine if they will work once your web is published, and publish your web to the Internet or your company's network. This section will help familiarize you with performing routine tasks in the FrontPage Explorer. The FrontPage Explorer allows you to view your web in several different ways.

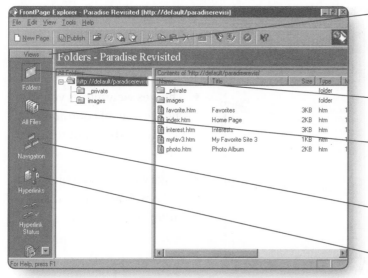

1. Click on a **Views button**. The corresponding view will appear in the right side of the FrontPage Explorer window.

✦ **Folders** view shows how the web content is organized.

✦ **All Files** view shows all of the files contained in the web and information about each one.

✦ **Navigation** view shows an organization chart of the web.

✦ **Hyperlinks** view shows links between pages inside the web and links to pages outside the web.

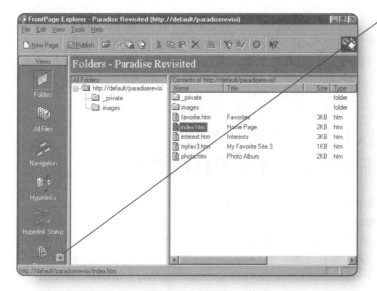

2. Click on the **down arrow** at the bottom right of the Views bar. The list of Views buttons will scroll down and an up arrow button will appear at the top right of the Views bar.

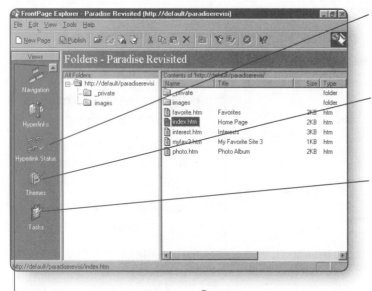

✦ **Hyperlink Status** view shows whether the hyperlinks contained in the web are linked properly to another page.

✦ **Themes** view allows you to choose a set of coordinated backgrounds and buttons for the web.

✦ **Tasks** view shows which parts of the web are finished and unfinished.

3. **Click** on the **up arrow** at the top right of the Views bar. The list of Views buttons will scroll up.

TIP

The Navigation View is one of the easiest views in which to perform most tasks.

EXPLORING THE FRONTPAGE EDITOR

The FrontPage Editor helps you design and edit your web pages. The FrontPage Editor displays text, graphics, and other page elements in WYSIWYG (What You See Is What You Get) format. While you're creating a page, you can see what it will look like when viewed on the Internet. You will first need to open the FrontPage Editor and familiarize yourself with its basic tools.

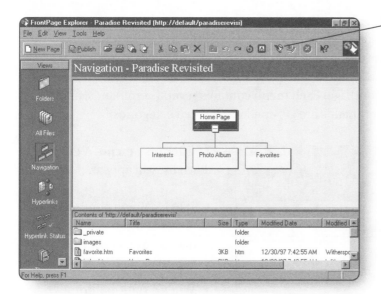

1. Click on the **FrontPage Editor button**. The FrontPage Editor will open with a blank page displayed.

Using Toolbars

The FrontPage Editor toolbar contains buttons that are shortcuts for many menu commands.

1. Place the **mouse pointer** over each toolbar button. A tool tip will appear telling you what function the button performs.

NOTE

Toolbar buttons are grouped into related functions and a bar separates groups. This makes it easier to find what you need on the toolbar quickly.

Using Menus

The FrontPage Editor and the FrontPage Explorer contain many menus. With them, you can execute any function in FrontPage. Each menu contains several commands, and these commands are grouped into related categories.

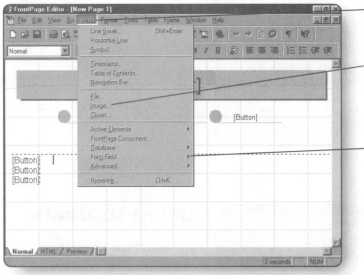

1. **Click** on a **menu**. A drop-down list will appear.

✦ When a menu command is followed by an ellipsis, a dialog box will appear if that command is selected.

✦ When a right-pointing arrowhead follows a menu command, another menu will appear when the mouse pointer is moved over the command.

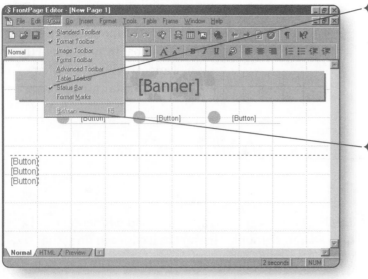

✦ When a menu command is preceded by a check mark, the command acts as a toggle. A check mark turns a function on, a missing check mark means the function is turned off.

✦ When a menu command is grayed out, it means the command is not available. You may need to perform some function to use the grayed out command.

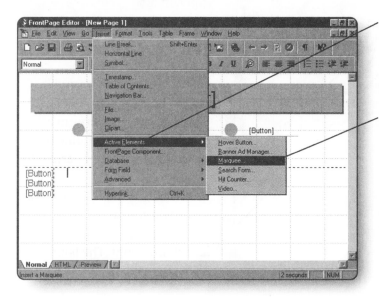

2. Place the **mouse pointer** over a **menu command** with a right-pointing arrowhead. A second menu will appear.

3. Move the **mouse pointer** to the right over a **command** on the second menu. The command will be highlighted.

4. Click on the **command**. The command will be executed.

Using Command Shortcuts

You may have noticed the keyboard shortcuts listed on the right side of each of the menus. You can use these shortcuts to open menus without clicking on them. As you become familiar with FrontPage, you may want to memorize these keyboard shortcuts. Not only will they help increase your productivity, but they will help decrease wrist strain caused by excessive mouse usage. The following table lists a few of the more common keyboard shortcuts that you may want to memorize.

To execute this command	Do this
Use FrontPage Help	Press the F1 key
Create a new page	Press the Ctrl and N keys simultaneously (Ctrl+N)
Open a different Web page	Press Ctrl+O
Save a Web page	Press Ctrl+S
Print a Web page	Press Ctrl+P
Delete selected text from a Web page	Press Ctrl+X
Make a copy of the selected text	Press Ctrl+C
Paste the copied text	Press Ctrl+V
Spell check a Web page	Press the F7 key

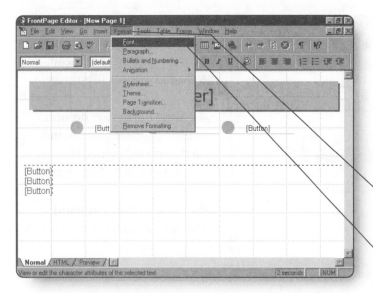

Working with Dialog Boxes

Dialog boxes group several related functions in one place. They allow you to perform a number of tasks regarding the menu command they pertain to.

1. Click on **Format**. The Format menu will appear.

2. Click on **Font**. The Font dialog box will appear.

✦ Select options by clicking on the arrow at either end of the vertical scroll bar to view the options, and then click on an option to select it.

✦ Turn features on and off by clicking on the check box to the left of the feature name.

✦ View the effect of the feature by looking at the preview (Sample) pane.

✦ Access a secondary dialog box by clicking on a button.

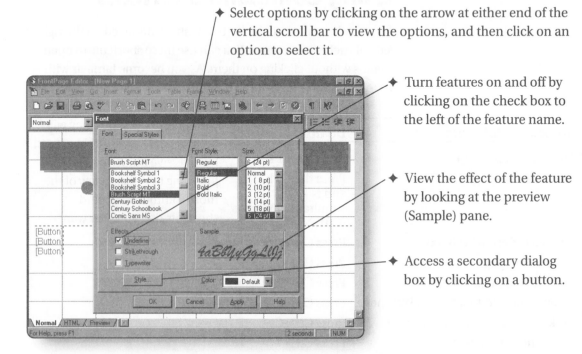

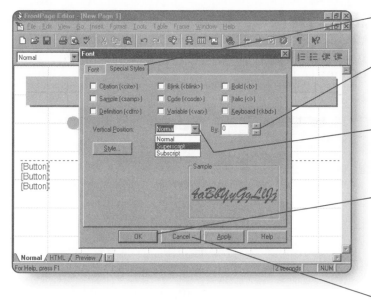

✦ Find more options by clicking on a tab.

✦ Adjust numbers and measurements by clicking on the up arrow and down arrow.

✦ Select options from drop-down lists by clicking on the down arrow.

3. **Click** on **OK**. The dialog box will close and the options will be applied to the web page.

TIP

Click on Cancel if you don't wish to alter the font at this time.

Using Scroll Bars

You will find two types of scroll bars in FrontPage: vertical scroll bars and horizontal scroll bars.

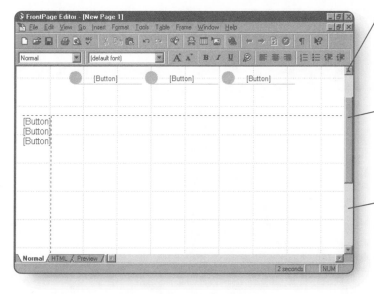

1. **Click** on the **arrow** at either end of the vertical scroll bar. The page will shift up or down one line at a time.

2. **Press** and **hold** the **mouse button** on the **scroll box** and **drag** it up or down. The page will shift up or down accordingly.

3. **Click** inside the **scroll bar**. The page will shift up or down one screen at a time.

GETTING HELP

If you are unfamiliar with a feature or function of FrontPage, there are a couple of places where you can get help.

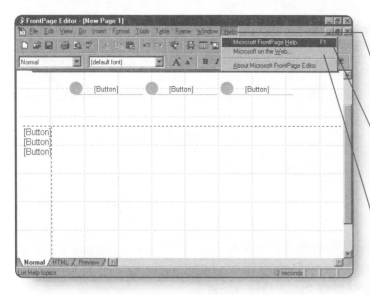

Searching the Help Topics

1. **Click** on **Help.** The Help menu will appear.

2. **Click** on **Microsoft FrontPage Help.** The Help Topics dialog box will appear with the Contents tab on top.

TIP

The Microsoft on the Web command connects to the Internet and accesses the Microsoft FrontPage Web site. This site offers product information, product support, and special offers.

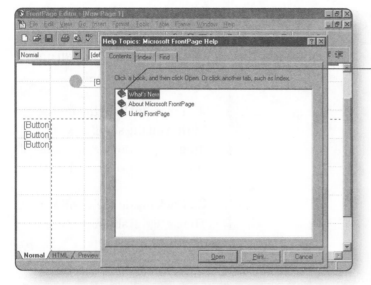

3. **Double-click** on the **Book icon** next to the topic that you want to know more about. The topic will expand to show the contents.

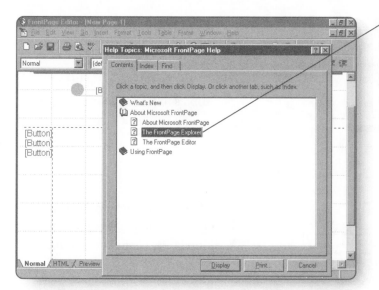

4. Double-click on the **item** about which you need more information. The associated help file will appear in a separate window.

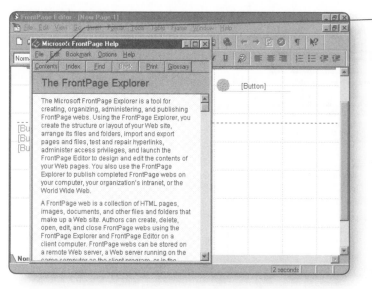

5. Click on **Contents**. The Help Topics dialog box will appear.

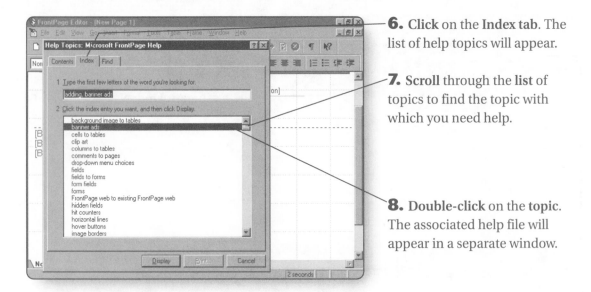

6. **Click** on the **Index tab**. The list of help topics will appear.

7. **Scroll** through the **list** of topics to find the topic with which you need help.

8. **Double-click** on the **topic**. The associated help file will appear in a separate window.

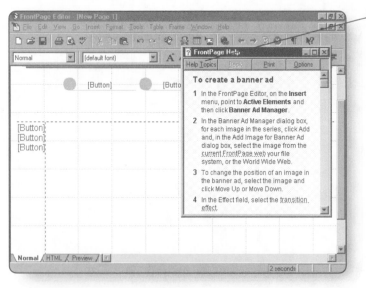

9. **Click** on the **Help Topics button**. The Help Topics Dialog box will appear.

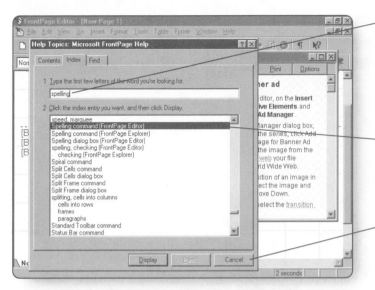

10. Type a **keyword** in the text box. The closest match will display in the list of topics.

NOTE

Double-click on a topic to display the associated help file.

11. Click on **Cancel**. The Help Topics dialog box will close.

Using the Help Button

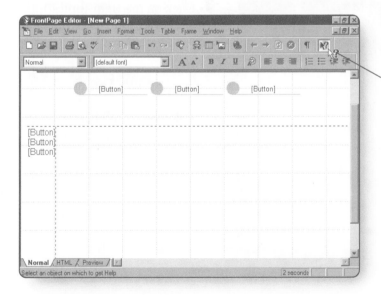

1. Click on the **Help button**. The mouse pointer will change to a pointer with a question mark.

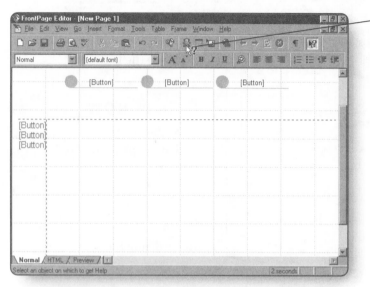

2. Click on the **item** about which you want more information. A help window will appear.

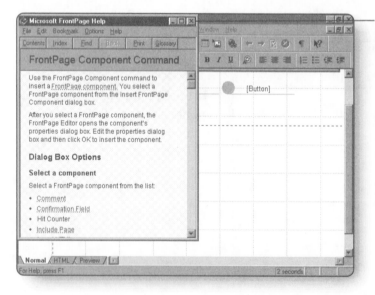

3. Click on the **Close button**. The help window will disappear.

TIP

You can find help inside dialog boxes by clicking on a question mark button or a Help button.

EXITING FRONTPAGE

When you are working in FrontPage, you are actually working with two windows: the FrontPage Explorer and the FrontPage Editor. Both of these windows will need to be closed.

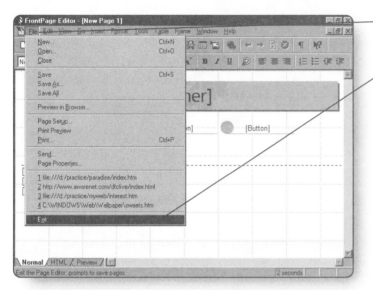

1. Click on **File**. The File menu will appear.

2. Click on **Exit**. The FrontPage Editor will close and the FrontPage Explorer will be displayed.

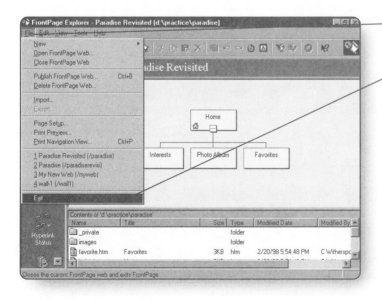

1. Click on **File**. The File menu will appear.

2. Click on **Exit**. The FrontPage Explorer will close.

2

Working with Pages in the FrontPage Explorer

The personal web you created in the FrontPage Explorer contains a Home Page (the main page of your web) and three pages that are attached (linked) to it. The Home Page is the introduction and starting place for your web (this is the first page that visitors will see when they access your Web site from the Internet). The pages attached to it cover the topics introduced in the Home Page in greater detail. This web will work well for you if you have three distinct topics that you want included in your web. If you want to include more than three topics, you will need to add additional pages with the FrontPage Explorer. In this chapter, you'll learn how to:

✦ Add and delete new pages

✦ Name and rename existing pages

✦ Move pages around in the FrontPage Explorer

ADDING A PAGE

The easiest way to add new pages to your web is with the Navigation view. By using the Navigation view, you can add pages so that they are automatically linked to the other pages in your web. This allows you to take advantage of the navigation controls that are part of the template you are using to build your web. But before you can add pages to your web, you will need to open FrontPage and have the FrontPage Explorer displayed on your screen. See Chapter 1 for help starting FrontPage.

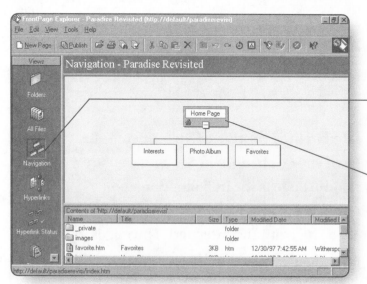

1. Click on the **Navigation button**. The Navigation view will appear.

2. Click on the **Home Page**. The page will be selected.

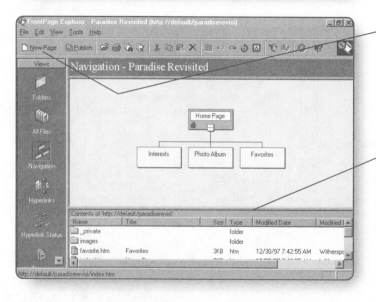

3. Click on the **New Page button**. A new page will be added to the web and linked to the Home Page.

TIP

To increase the size of the Files pane, click and hold the bar between the Files and Navigation panes and drag the bar upwards.

DELETING A PAGE

As you are building or updating, you may find that you have pages that you no longer need, or you may not want to give your visitors access to certain Web pages. The easiest way to get rid of anything is to delete it. FrontPage allows you to delete pages from your web without completely losing all your work.

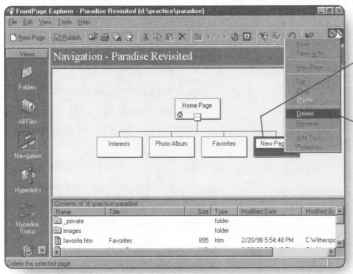

1. Right-click on the **page** that you want removed from the web. A menu will appear.

2. Click on **Delete**. The Delete Page dialog box will appear.

3. Click on the **Remove this page from all navigation bars option button**. The option will be selected.

4. Click on **OK**. The page will be deleted from the web structure but will still be available for use in FrontPage.

TIP

If you want to completely remove the page from your computer, select the Delete this page from the FrontPage web option button.

Using the Private Folder

You could leave pages that are removed from the navigation structure where they are in the web filing system. But if you do this, you may accidentally publish this page to your site, where inquisitive web surfers may find it. To keep the page for future use and to make it unavailable to visitors, place the page in the private folder.

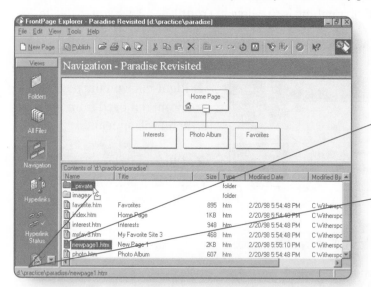

1. Press and hold the mouse button on the file in the Files pane. The file will be selected.

2. Drag the file to the _private folder. The file will be available for you to use but will not be accessible to anyone visiting your Web site.

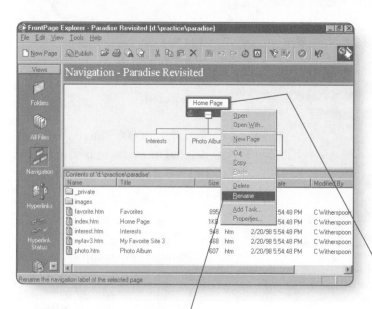

NAMING A PAGE

The titles that FrontPage gives to each of the pages in the web are examples of how you might title your own web pages. New pages that you add are called, simply enough, New Page. You'll want to give each of your pages a new title that describes its unique content.

1. Press the right mouse button (right-click) on the Home Page. A shortcut menu will appear.

2. Click on Rename. The page title will be highlighted.

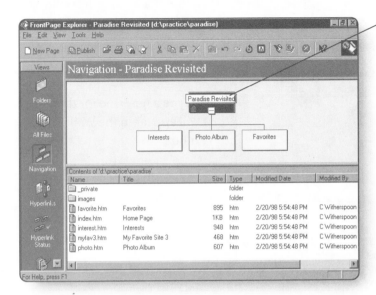

3. Type a new **title** for the page.

4. **Press** the **Enter key**. You can do the same for the other pages.

RENAMING YOUR WEB

If you are not satisfied with the original title that you gave your web, you can change it. Remember to make your title appropriate to your web. This is the title that visitors will see in the title bar of the Web browser that they are using.

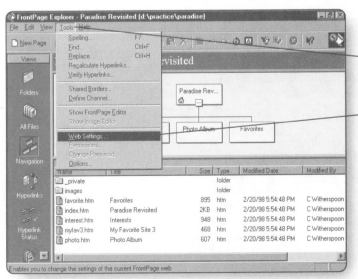

1. **Click** on **Tools**. The Tools menu will appear.

2. **Click** on **Web Settings**. The FrontPage Web Settings dialog box will appear with the Configuration tab displayed.

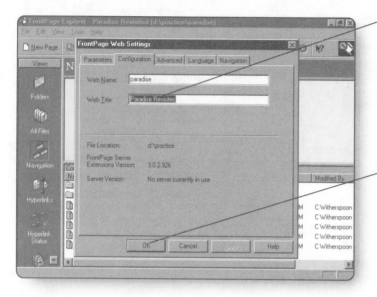

3. Select the text in the Web Title: text box. The text will be highlighted.

4. Type a new title for the web. It will appear in the Web Title: text box.

5. Click on OK. The web will be renamed.

Moving Pages Using Drag-and-Drop

You may want to move pages around to change the structure of your web.

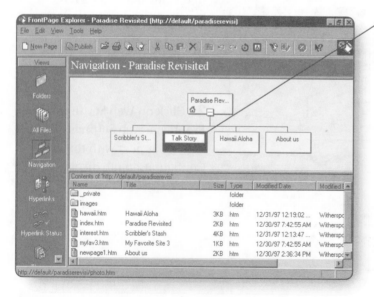

1. Press and hold the mouse button on the page to be moved. The page will be selected.

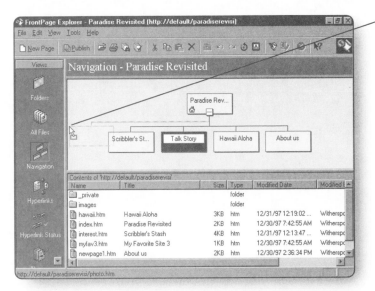

2. **Drag** the **page** to a side of your chart. The page will turn into an outline.

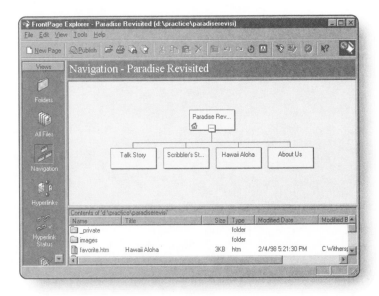

3. **Release** the **mouse button**. The page will be moved.

3

Working with Pages in the FrontPage Editor

When you open a new page in the FrontPage Editor, the insertion point will be at the upper-left corner of the page. This is your beginning point. You can begin typing on this blank page just as you would in a word processing program. Once you've added a few words to get your page started, you may want to edit the text, add graphics for a little color, and move some things around. In this chapter, you'll learn how to:

✦ Add, copy, and move text and graphics

✦ Work with clip art

✦ Apply styles to paragraphs

✦ Undo mistakes

OPENING A PAGE FROM THE FRONTPAGE EXPLORER

In the first chapter, you learned how to get started building your web. You did this by using the Personal Web template. Now that you have a structure on which to hang your web, it's time to add some content to each of the pages. But first, you will need to know how to open individual pages in the FrontPage Explorer.

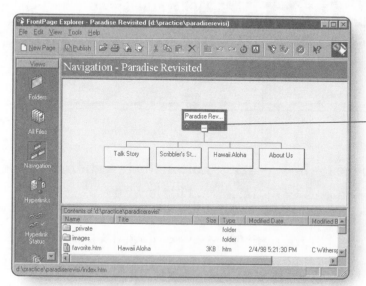

1. Double-click on the **Home page** in the Navigation view. The page will appear in the FrontPage Editor window.

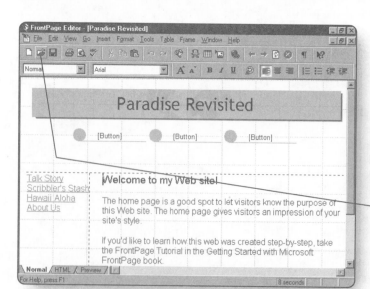

Opening a Page from the FrontPage Editor

You may wish to work on a different page while in the FrontPage Editor. To switch pages, do the following.

1. Click on the **Open button**. The Open dialog box will appear.

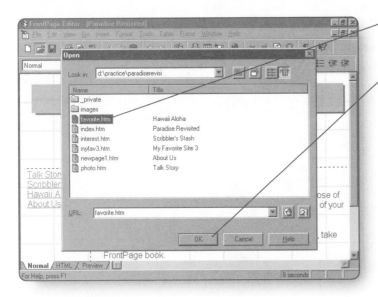

2. **Click** on a **page**. The page will be selected.

3. **Click** on **OK**. The page will appear in the FrontPage Editor.

INSERTING TEXT AND GRAPHICS

Text and graphics make up the largest portion of a web. As you build your web, you will want to add additional text and insert pictures. FrontPage offers you over 1600 pictures from which to choose, making it quick and easy to give your pages color.

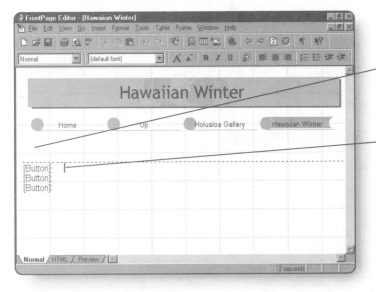

Adding Text

1. **Open** the **page** that you want to work on. The page will appear in the FrontPage Editor.

2. **Click** on the **blank area** to the right of the [Button]. The insertion bar will appear on the page.

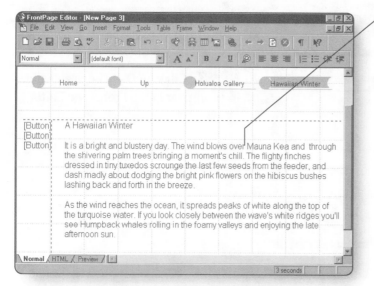

3. **Type** some **text**. You may wish to type a few sentences about what you want to do with your web. You may want to tell a story, talk about your profession, or share your hobbies.

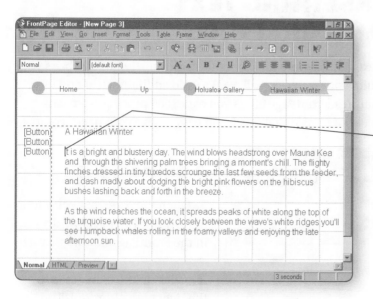

Adding Clip Art

You may wish to insert a picture or graphic to go along with the text you've written.

1. **Click** on the **area** where you wish to insert a picture. The insertion bar will appear.

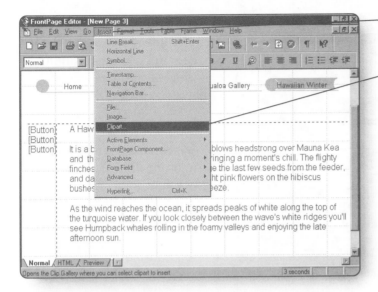

2. Click on **Insert**. The Insert menu will appear.

3. Click on **Clipart**. The Microsoft Clip Gallery dialog box will open with the Clip Art tab displayed.

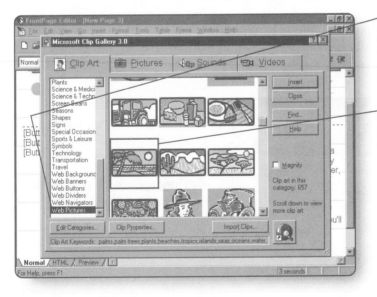

4. Click on the **category** of Clip Art for which you are looking. The clip art in that category will appear in the preview pane.

5. Click on the **picture** that you want to add to the Web page. The picture will be selected.

6. **Click** on the **Insert button**. The picture will be added to the page at the selected position.

SELECTING TEXT

Many text editing commands require that you select text first. This section will show you how to select text using several methods.

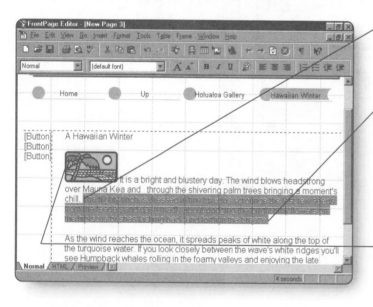

1. **Click** and **hold** at the **beginning** of the text you want to select.

2. **Drag** the **mouse pointer** to the **end** of the text you want to select.

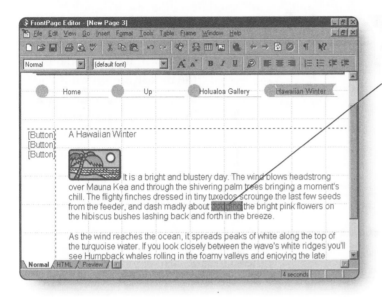

Using Shortcuts to Select Text

✦ Select one word by clicking twice on the word.

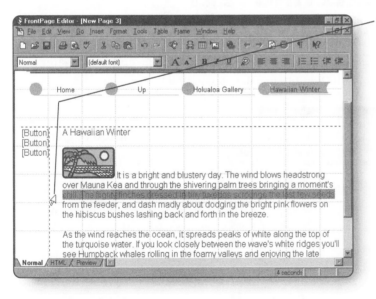

✦ Select a line by placing the mouse pointer on the left margin and clicking once next to the line.

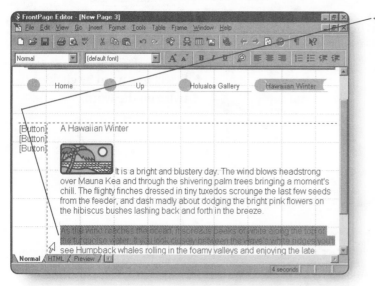

✦ Select several lines by placing the mouse pointer on the left margin, and press and hold the mouse button while you drag the mouse pointer next to each line that you want to select.

DELETING TEXT AND GRAPHICS

When you've placed something on a page and decide later that you don't want to use it, you can delete it.

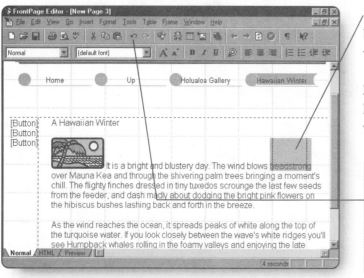

1. Select the **text** or **graphic** to be deleted. The text or graphic will be highlighted.

2. Press the **Delete key** on the keyboard. The text or graphic will be deleted.

TIP

You can delete text and graphics immediately after you have placed them on a page by clicking on the Undo button.

WORKING WITH TEXT AND GRAPHICS

The text and graphics on a page can be moved or copied so that several duplicates appear on the page.

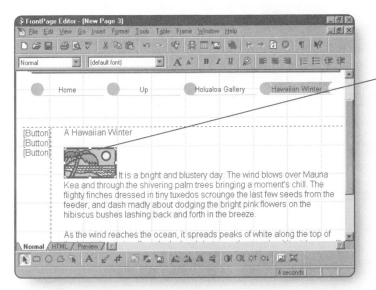

Moving Text and Graphics

1. **Select** the **text** or **graphic** to be moved. The text or graphic will be highlighted.

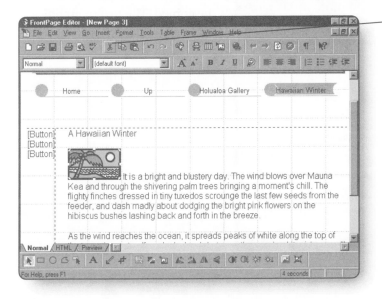

2. **Click** on the **Cut button**. The text or graphic will disappear and be stored in the Windows clipboard.

3. **Click** on the **place** where you want the text or graphic moved. The insertion bar will appear.

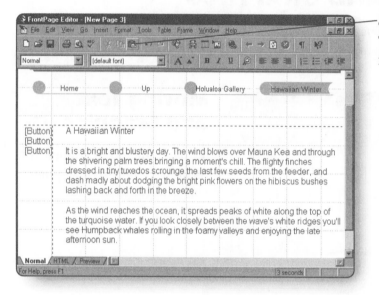

4. **Click** on the **Paste button**. The text or graphic will appear in the new position.

Copying Text and Graphics

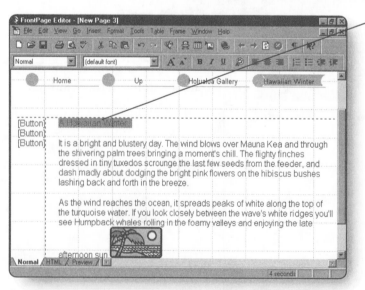

1. **Select** the **text** or **graphic** to be copied. The text or graphic will be highlighted.

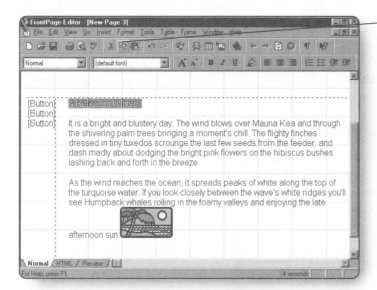

2. **Click** on the **Copy button**. The text or graphic will be stored in the Windows clipboard.

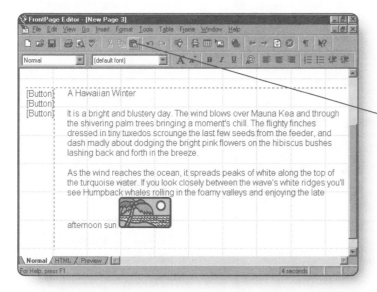

3. **Click** on the **place** where you want to put a copy of the text or graphic. The insertion bar will appear.

4. **Click** on the **Paste button**. The text or graphic will be copied to the new position.

USING STYLES

FrontPage uses HTML styles that can be interpreted by any Web browser to display formatted text. It is a good idea to use paragraph styles to format text.

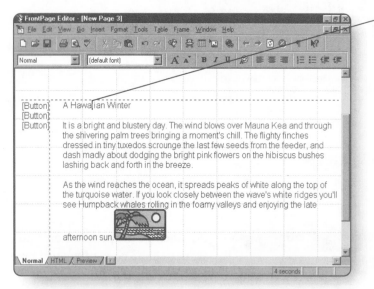

1. **Click** in the **paragraph** that you want to format.

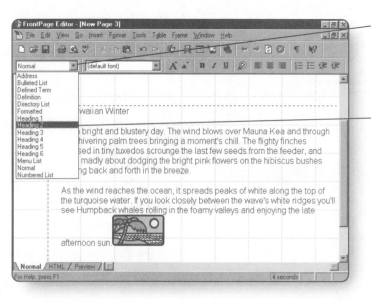

2. **Click** on the **down arrow** in the Change Style field. A drop-down list of style options will appear.

3. **Click** on a **style** that you want to use. The paragraph will appear in the style that you chose.

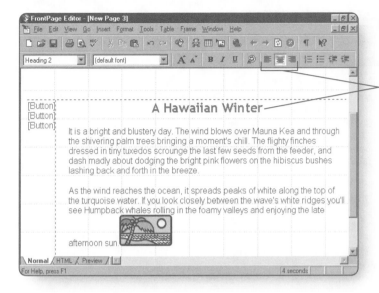

Using Shortcuts to Format Text

✦ To change the paragraph alignment, click on the Left, Center, or Right buttons.

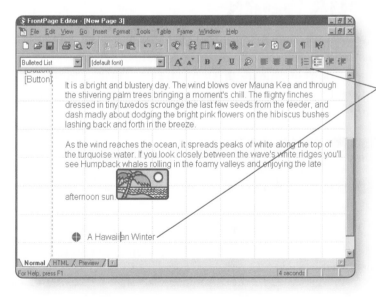

✦ To create a list, click on the Numbered List or Bulleted List buttons. To learn more about lists, see Chapter 6, "Creating and Formatting Lists."

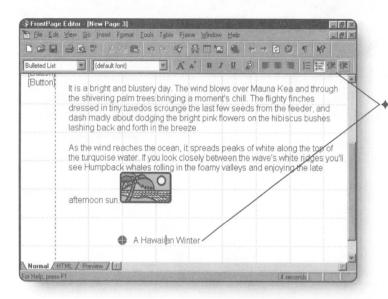

✦ To change the left margin for a paragraph, click on the Decrease Indent or Increase Indent buttons.

UNDOING AND REDOING YOUR WORK

As you are working on a page, you'll be making lots of changes. There will be times when you make a change and then decide that you don't like the result. Or maybe you'll make a mistake and want to undo that mistake. Here's how to undo and redo a series of actions.

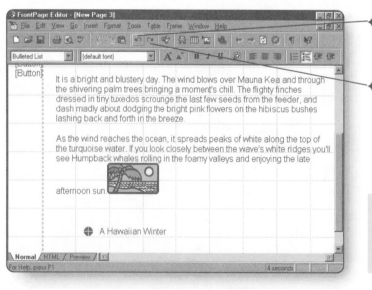

✦ Click on the Undo button to reverse the last action you performed.

✦ Click on the Redo button to reverse the effect of the last Undo command that you performed.

NOTE

You can undo and redo the last 30 actions.

4 Viewing and Saving Your Web

As you work with your web, you will want to see how your work is progressing. You can do this by either previewing your web or by printing the Web pages. You'll also want to know if your web displays properly in a variety of Web browsers. Also, you'll need to make sure that all your words are spelled correctly. Then, to make sure you don't lose all your hard work, you'll need to save your web. In this chapter, you'll learn how to:

✦ Save a web

✦ Spell check a web

✦ View a web before you publish it on the Internet

✦ Print different elements of a web

SAVING YOUR WEB

The importance of saving your work can't be stressed enough. Computers are subject to a number of factors that can cause them to crash. Crashes may be caused by something as simple as an electrical surge or outage, or by something more complex, such as a hardware problem. To protect yourself from lost work, save your work every few minutes.

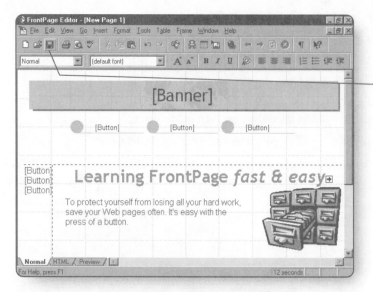

Saving Individual Web Pages

1. Click on the **Save button**. The Save As dialog box will appear.

NOTE

The Save As dialog box only appears the first time you save a Web page.

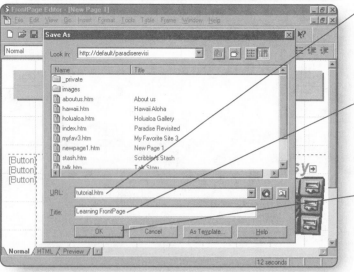

2. Type a **file name** for the Web page in the URL: text box. Use a file name that is eight characters or less with the extension .htm.

3. Type a **title** for the page in the Title: text box. Use a word or short phrase that describes what will be found on the page.

4. Click on OK. The Save Embedded Files dialog box will appear if there are embedded files (such as graphical images) in the page.

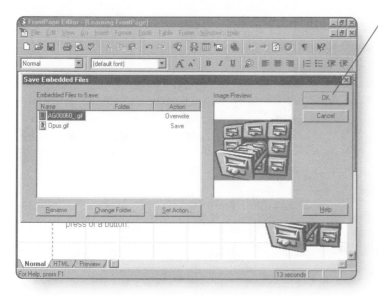

5. **Click** on **OK**. The Web page will be saved with the current FrontPage web on which you are working.

Saving Web Pages Under a Different Name

1. **Click** on **File**. The File menu will appear.

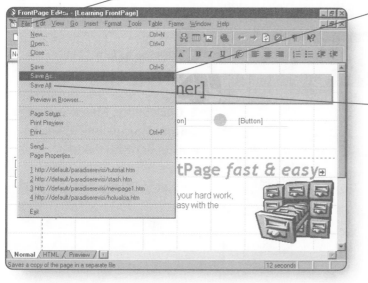

2. **Click** on **Save As**. The Save As dialog box will appear.

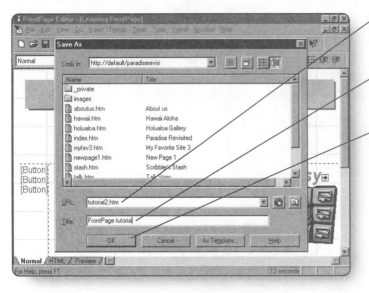

3. **Type** a new **file name** for the Web page in the URL: text box.

4. **Type** a new **title** for the Web page in the Title: text box.

5. **Click** on **OK**. The Web page will be saved with a different file name.

CHECKING YOUR SPELLING

Before you publish your web on the Internet or your company's intranet, you'll want to check to make sure that you have spelled every word correctly. Spelling errors can make even the best Web site look bad.

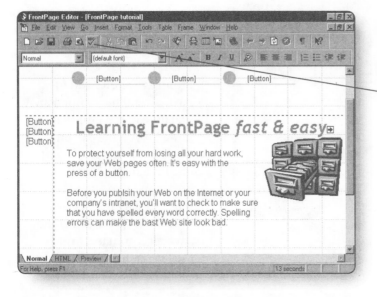

Checking an Individual Page

1. **Click** on the **Check Spelling button.** The Spelling dialog box will appear with the first misspelled word displayed in the Not in Dictionary: text box.

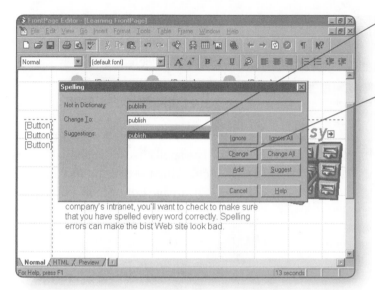

2. **Click** on the **correct spelling** in the Suggestions: text box. The word will be selected.

3. **Click** on the **Change button**. The next misspelled word will appear in the Not in Dictionary: text box.

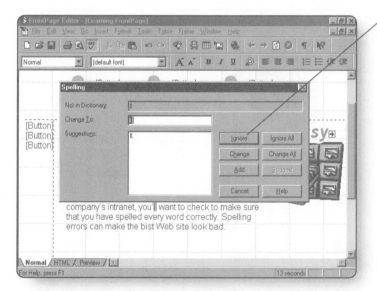

4. **Click** on the **Ignore button**. The word will be left as is and the next misspelled word will appear in the Not in Dictionary: text box.

TIP

The misspelled word will also be highlighted on the Web page. This will help you determine how to correct the error.

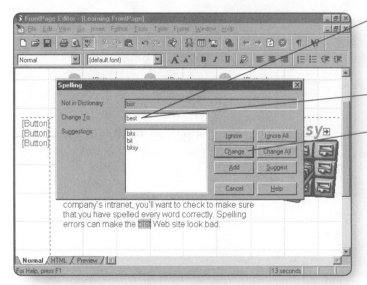

5. **Click** in the **Change to: text box**. The word in the text box will be selected.

6. **Type** the **correct word**.

7. **Click** on the **Change button**. The spell checker will finish checking the document and the FrontPage Editor dialog box will appear.

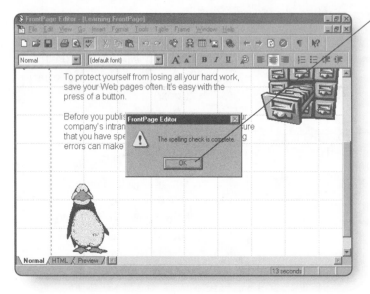

8. **Click** on **OK**. The spell check will be completed.

NOTE

Now would be a good time to save your Web page.

Checking the Entire Web

After you get comfortable working with FrontPage and have a clearer idea of what you want to do with your web, you'll begin working with multiple pages at one time. When you get to this point, you won't want to spell check each individual page because of the amount of time this will take. It is possible to do one spell check on the entire web.

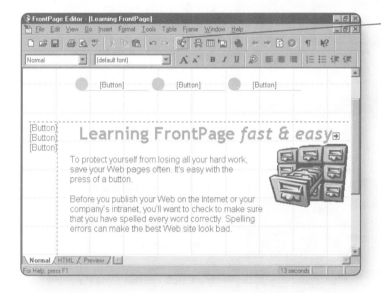

1. **Click** on the **Show FrontPage Explorer button** on the FrontPage Editor toolbar. The FrontPage Explorer will appear.

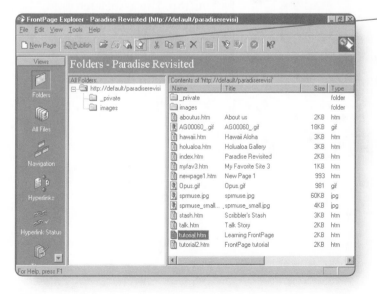

2. **Click** on the **Cross File Spelling button**. The Spelling dialog box will appear.

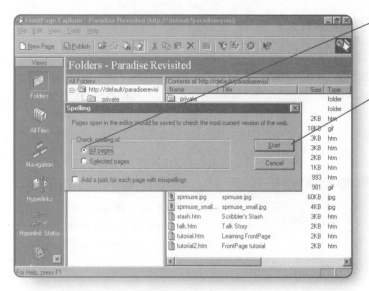

3. Click on the **All pages option button**. The option will be selected.

4. Click on **Start**. Another Spelling dialog box will appear showing the progress of the spell check and the pages that contain misspelled words.

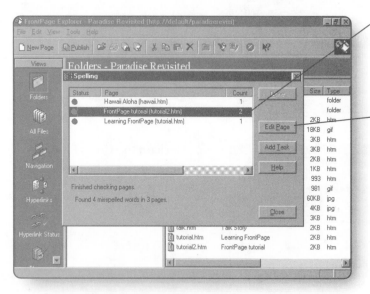

5. Click on the **page** that contains the misspelling that you want to correct. The page will be selected.

6. Click on the **Edit Page button**. The associated page will appear in the FrontPage Editor window with the first misspelled word displayed in the Spelling dialog box.

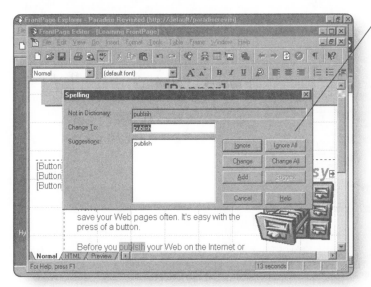

7. Make the appropriate **corrections**. When you have finished with the corrections, the Continue with the next document? dialog box will appear.

NOTE

For help using the spell checker on an individual page, see the previous section, "Checking an Individual Page."

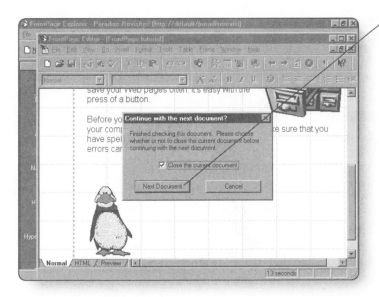

8. Click on the **Next Document button**. The next Web page that contains misspellings will appear in the FrontPage Editor Window.

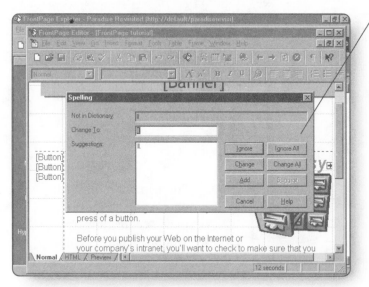

9. **Make** the appropriate **corrections**. When you have finished with the corrections to all of the listed pages, the Finish checking documents dialog box will appear.

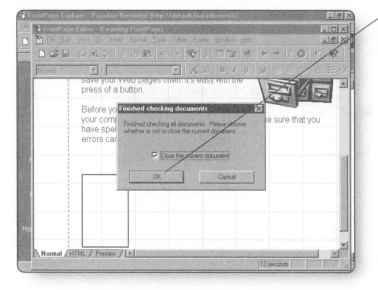

10. **Click** on **OK**. The FrontPage Editor window will be blank.

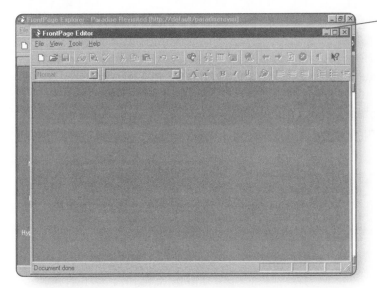

11. Minimize the **FrontPage Editor window**. The FrontPage Explorer window will appear with the Spelling dialog box displayed.

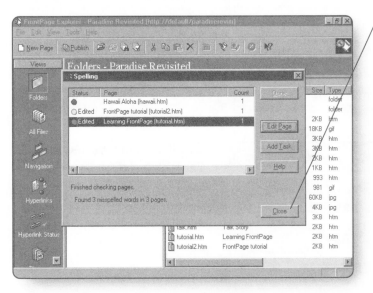

12. Click on the **Close button**. The spell check will be complete.

PREVIEWING YOUR WEB

Before you publish your page, you'll want to make sure that you are satisfied with the way it looks in a Web browser. If you have Internet Explorer 3.0 or higher installed on your computer, you can easily preview any Web page from the FrontPage Editor window.

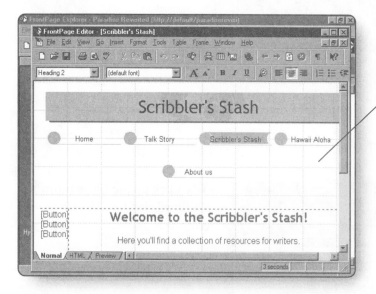

Previewing from the FrontPage Editor

1. **Open** the **Web page** that you want to preview in the FrontPage Editor. The page will appear.

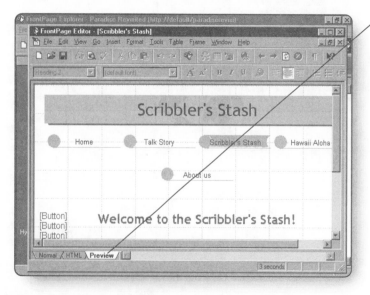

2. **Click** on the **Preview tab**. The Web page appears in the Preview window as it would in the version of Internet Explorer that you have on your computer.

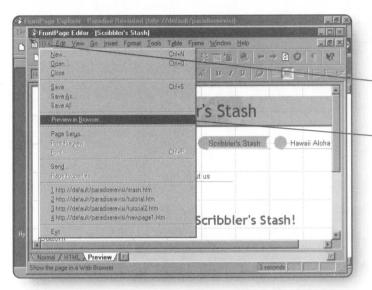

Previewing from a Web Browser

1. **Click** on **File**. The File menu will appear.

2. **Click** on **Preview in Browser**. The Preview in Browser dialog box will appear.

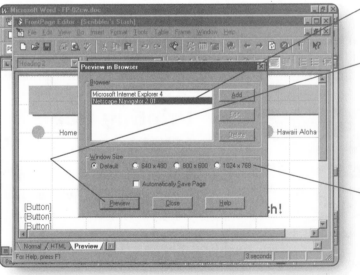

3. **Click** on a **Web browser**. The Web browser will be selected.

4. **Click** on **Preview**.

TIP

You can experiment with how your page will look when viewed in different screen resolutions by choosing one of the option buttons in the Window Size selection area.

The Web page will appear in the selected browser.

PRINTING YOUR WEB

You may want to print copies of your Web page. By printing copies of your page, you'll have a permanent copy of your web. You may also want to print a chart that shows how your web is organized. This section will show you how easy printing can be.

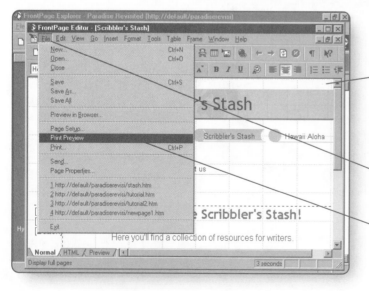

Printing Web Pages

1. **Open** the **Web page** that you want to print. The Web page will appear in the FrontPage Editor window.

2. **Click** on **File**. The File menu will appear.

3. **Click** on **Print Preview**. The Preview window will appear showing how the page will look when printed.

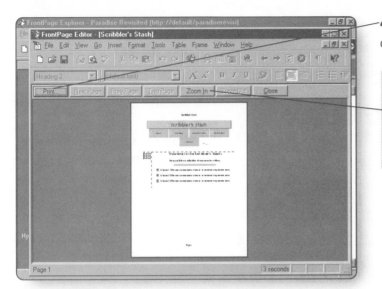

4. **Click** on **Print**. The Print dialog box will appear.

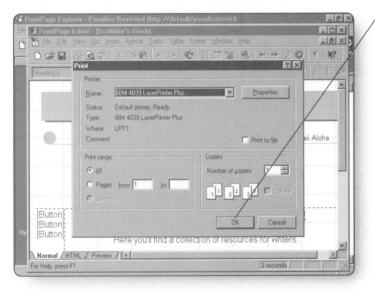

5. **Click** on **OK**. The Web page will be printed.

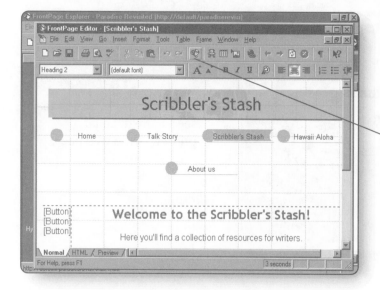

Printing a Site Map

You may want to print an organizational chart of your web.

1. **Click** on the **Show FrontPage Explorer button**. The FrontPage Explorer will appear.

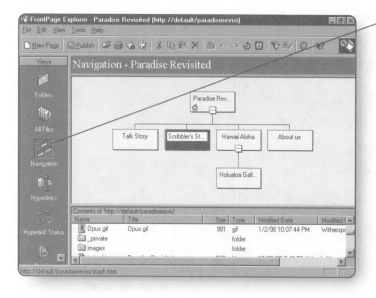

2. **Click** on the **Navigation button**. The Navigation view will appear in the FrontPage Explorer window.

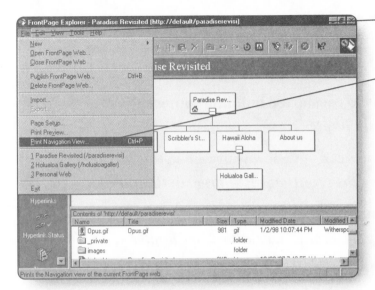

3. **Click** on **File**. The File menu will appear.

4. **Click** on **Print Navigation View**. The Print Dialog Box will appear.

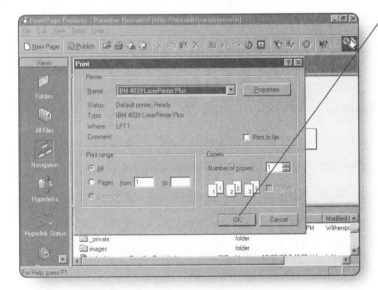

5. **Click** on **OK**. An organizational chart of the web will print.

PART I REVIEW QUESTIONS

1. What is the easiest way to get started building your web? *See "Opening a Web" in Chapter 1.*

2. How many different ways can you view your web in the FrontPage Explorer? *See "Viewing the FrontPage Explorer" in Chapter 1.*

3. How do you switch from the FrontPage Explorer to the FrontPage Editor? *See "Exploring the FrontPage Editor" in Chapter 1.*

4. What are the three different places where you can find help using FrontPage? *See "Getting Help" in Chapter 1.*

5. How do you rename your web? *See "Renaming Your Web" in Chapter 2.*

6. Which toolbar buttons allow you to move text and graphics around on a Web page? *See "Inserting Text and Graphics" in Chapter 3.*

7. How many actions can be successively undone while you are editing a Web page? *See "Undoing and Redoing Your Work" in Chapter 3.*

8. If you have several Web pages open in the FrontPage Editor, how do you save all of them at one time? *See "Saving Your Web" in Chapter 4.*

9. How does using the spell checker inside the FrontPage Editor differ from using the spell checker inside the FrontPage Explorer? *See "Checking Your Spelling" in Chapter 4.*

10. How many different ways can you preview a Web page? *See "Previewing Your Web" in Chapter 4.*

PART II

Expanding Your Web

.gif
.jpg
ey.gif
a.jpg
ntpag.gi
ish.jpg
respond.gi
shark.gif
sunset.gif

URL: imag

HTML Preview

5 Designing Your Web

FrontPage contains many cool features and functions that make it easy to create a professional look for your web. You can use the built-in themes to give your web a consistent look. FrontPage automatically builds navigation controls that make it easy for visitors to navigate through your site. You can even use some of the same page transition effects that you may have seen in some presentation programs, such as Microsoft PowerPoint. Your friends will think you spent months building such an awesome Web site, and only you will know the truth. In this chapter, you'll learn how to:

✦ Use themes to give your web a professional look

✦ Apply navigation controls to a web

✦ Add page transition effects

GIVING YOUR WEB A THEME

FrontPage includes over 50 themes to help you make your Web site more attractive. Each theme contains color coordinated and graphically pleasing fonts, bullets, banners, and navigation bars. You don't need to be a graphic designer to make your web look good. Themes can be applied to an entire web or to individual pages, or, if you want to create your own look, you can choose not to use any of the themes that come with FrontPage.

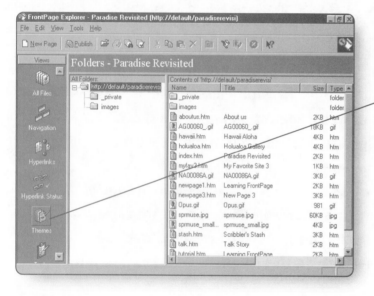

Applying a Theme to the Entire Web

1. Click on the **Themes button** on the View bar. The Themes dialog box will appear.

2. **Click** on the **Use Selected Theme: option button**. The option will be selected.

3. **Click** on a **Theme**. Each theme contains the same elements (banners, buttons, text colors), but different themes use different graphical images for each element. The selected theme will appear in the Theme Preview: pane.

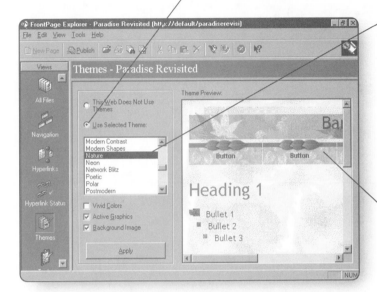

NOTE

As you select different themes and display options, the image in the preview pane will change. Use the preview pane to see how your web will look before you make a final decision.

4. **Click** on **Vivid Colors** to use bright colored text and graphics on certain theme components. A check will appear in the box.

5. **Click** on **Active Graphics** to animate certain theme components. A check will appear in the box.

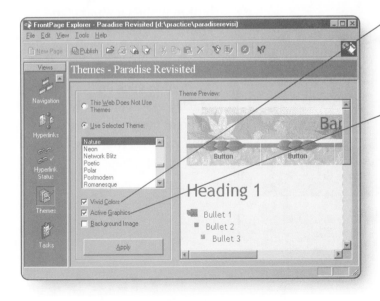

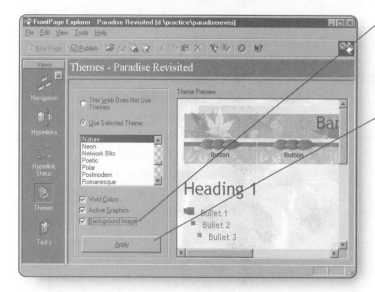

6. Click on **Background Image** to use a patterned background on Web pages. A check will appear in the box.

7. Click on **Apply**. The theme will be applied to the entire web.

Applying a Theme to an Individual Web Page

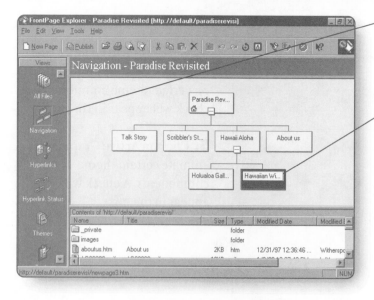

1. Click on the **Navigation button** in the View bar of the FrontPage Explorer. The Navigation view will appear.

2. Double-click on the **page** to which you want to apply a different theme. The page will appear in the FrontPage Editor.

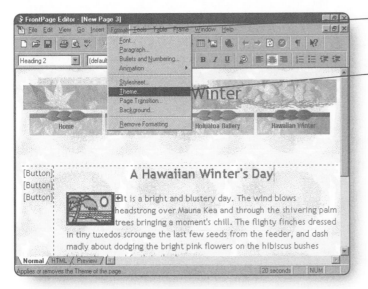

3. Click on **Format**. The Format menu will appear.

4. Click on **Theme**. The Choose Theme dialog box will appear.

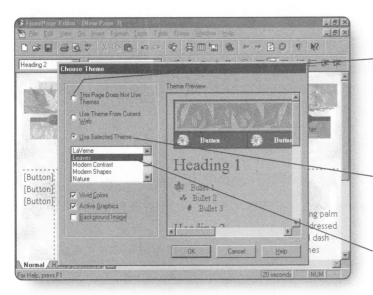

5. Click on the **Use Selected Theme: option button**. The option will be selected.

6. Click on a **Theme**. The selected theme will appear in the Theme Preview: window.

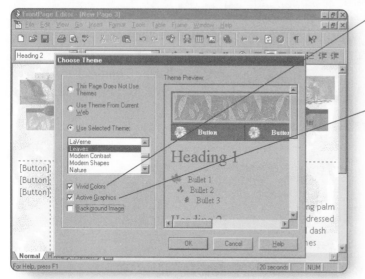

7. Click on **Vivid Colors** to use bright colored text and graphics on certain theme components. A check will appear in the box.

8. Click on **Active Graphics** to animate certain theme components. A check will appear in the box.

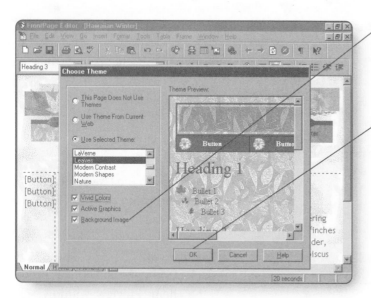

9. Click on **Background Image** to use a patterned background on Web pages. A check will appear in the box.

10. Click on **OK**. The theme will be applied to the individual Web page.

SETTING BORDER FRAMES

Border frames allow you to add text, graphics, or navigation controls on one page and have that information appear on all the pages in a web.

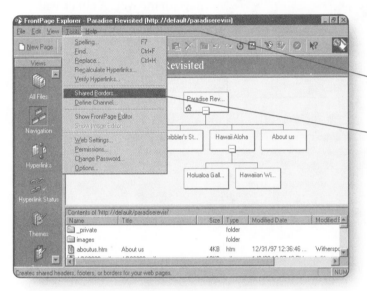

1. Open the FrontPage Explorer.

2. Click on Tools. The Tools menu will appear.

3. Click on Shared Borders. The Shared Borders dialog box will appear.

4. Click on Top to add a frame along the top of every page in the web. A check will appear in the box.

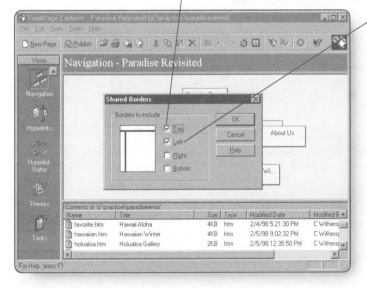

5. Click on Left to add a frame along the left side of every page in the web. A check will appear in the box.

NOTE

You must enable the top frame in order to view the banners that FrontPage automatically applies to each page when working with a theme.

6. **Click** on **Right** to add a frame along the right side of every page in the web. A check will appear in the box.

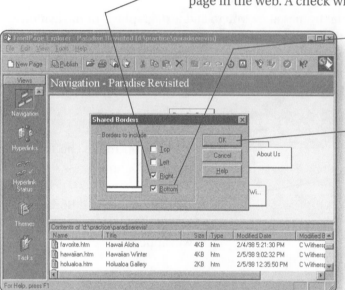

7. **Click** on **Bottom** to add a frame along the bottom of every page in the web. A check will appear in the box.

8. **Click** on **OK**. The border frames will be applied to the entire web.

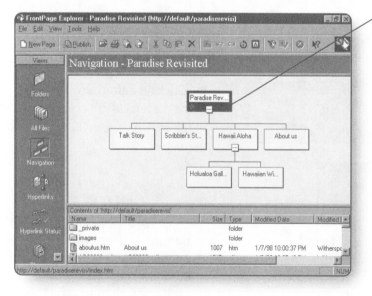

9. **Open** any **page** in the web. The page will appear in the FrontPage Editor.

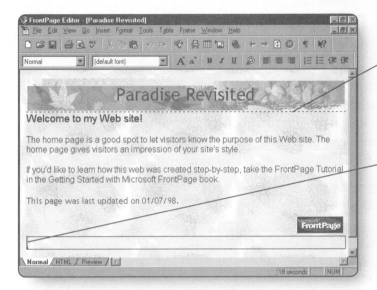

Shared borders are separated from the main part of a Web page by a dotted line.

10. **Click** inside the **shared border** to which you want to add content. The shared border will appear as a solid line and the pointer will appear in the selected border.

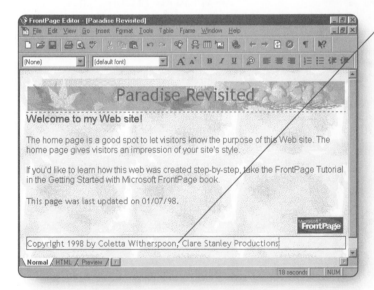

11. **Enter** the **content** that you want to appear on all pages in the web. The bottom border is a good place to put copyright information to protect your page, or your e-mail address so that visitors to your site can send you a message.

APPLYING NAVIGATION BUTTONS

One of the more confusing aspects of designing a Web site is adding navigation buttons that help visitors find their way around. If you had to add each navigation control to each page individually, you could easily miss a link to a page or you could link a navigation button to the wrong page. If your visitors can't navigate your site correctly, they'll lose interest and find another site. FrontPage takes the hassle out of building navigation controls by doing most of the work for you.

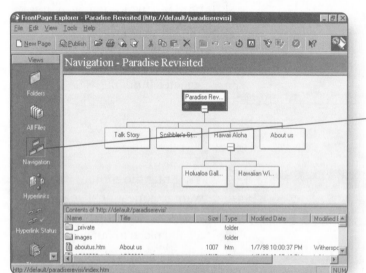

1. **Click** on the **Navigation button** in the View bar of the FrontPage Explorer. The Navigation view will appear.

2. **Double-click** on the **page** to which you want to add a navigation bar. The page will appear in the FrontPage Editor window.

3. **Click** on the **place** where you want to add the navigation bar. The insertion bar will appear in the selected place.

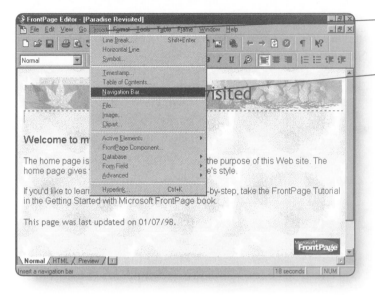

4. **Click** on **Insert**. The Insert menu will appear.

5. **Click** on **Navigation Bar**. The Navigation Bar Properties dialog box will appear.

6. **Click** on one of the **option buttons** from the Hyperlinks to include section of the dialog box. You will want to choose the option that corresponds to the page level you want to appear in the Navigation Bar:

✦ **Parent level.** Displays navigation controls to the pages that are above the selected page in the Navigation view organization chart.

✦ **Same level.** Displays navigation controls to the pages that are on the same level as the selected page in the Navigation view organization chart.

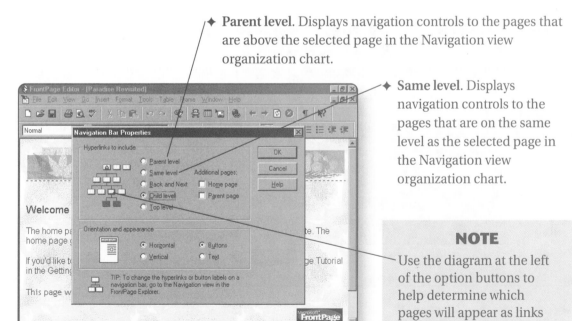

NOTE

Use the diagram at the left of the option buttons to help determine which pages will appear as links in the Navigation Bar.

✦ **Back and Next**. Displays navigation controls to the pages that are to the right and left of the selected page in the Navigation view organization chart.

✦ **Child level**. Displays navigation controls to the pages that are below the selected page in the Navigation view organization chart.

✦ **Top level**. Displays navigation controls to pages that are on the same level as the Home page for the web in the Navigation view organization chart.

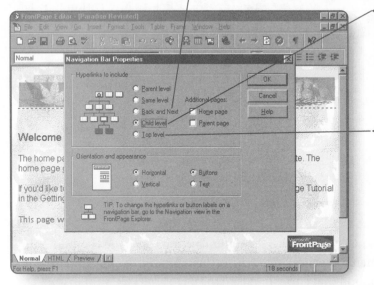

7. **Click** on **Home page** to add a navigation button to the Home page for the web. A check will appear in the box.

8. **Click** on **Parent page** to add a navigation button to the page above the selected page. A check will appear in the box.

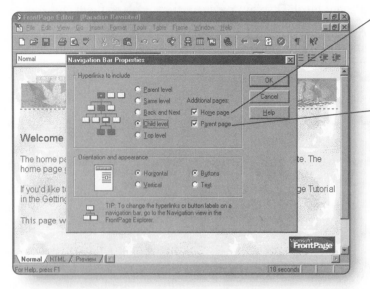

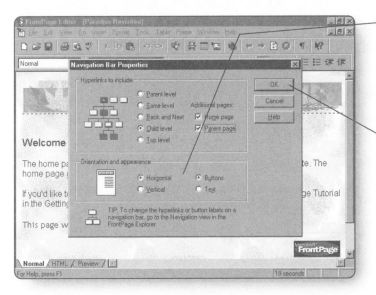

9. **Click** on an **option button** to select the orientation of the navigation controls. The option will be selected and the preview to the left will change accordingly.

10. **Click** on **OK**. The navigation bar will be added to the page.

ADDING PAGE TRANSITIONS

With the introduction of Dynamic HTML, the latest generation of Web browsers can now handle special page transition effects such as fades, wipes, dissolves, and splits. You may have seen these transition effects used in slide show presentations. Here's how you can add these same types of transitions to your Web pages.

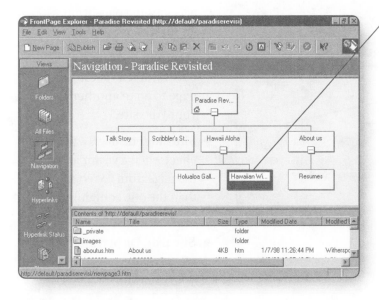

1. **Open** the **page** to which you want to apply a transition effect. The page will appear in the FrontPage Editor.

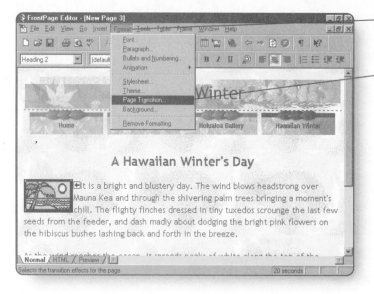

2. **Click** on **Format**. The Format menu will appear.

3. **Click** on **Page Transition**. The Page Transitions dialog box will appear.

4. **Click** on the **down arrow** next to the Event: list box. A drop-down list will appear.

5. **Click** on the **event** where you want the page transition to occur.

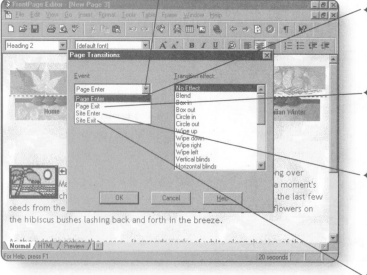

✦ **Page Enter** displays a transition effect when a visitor accesses the page from another page in your Web site.

✦ **Page Exit** displays a transition effect when a visitor exits the page to go to another page in your Web site.

✦ **Site Enter** displays a transition effect when a visitor accesses the page from a Web site other than the one containing the page.

✦ **Site Exit**. Displays a transition effect when a visitor exits your Web site.

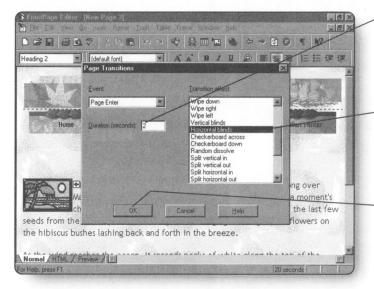

6. Type the **number of seconds** that you want the transition effect to last in the Duration (seconds): text box.

7. Click on the **Transition effect** that you want to use with the page. The transition effect will be selected.

8. Click on OK. The transition effect will be applied to the page.

NOTE

To preview the transition effect, you will need to open the page in a Web browser that is compatible with Dynamic HTML, such as Internet Explorer 4.0.

6 Creating and Formatting Lists

You can find lists in almost every part of your daily life. At home you put together to-do lists and grocery lists. At work, the boss may hand out an agenda before a meeting or you may read a procedure manual that lists the steps it takes to perform a task. On the Internet, you'll find lists on some of the Web pages that you visit. FrontPage makes it easy to format a number of different types of lists. In this chapter, you'll learn how to:

✦ Create and edit lists

✦ Format different types of lists

✦ Enable collapsible lists

✦ Change the graphical bullets used in a list

CREATING A SIMPLE LIST

You can create two types of simple lists in FrontPage: bulleted lists and numbered lists. Bulleted lists consist of a group of unordered items. Numbered lists consist of items that must be in a particular order, such as the steps required to perform a task. This section will show you how to format a simple list and how to add items after the main list has been created.

1. Open the **page** where the list will be located. The page will appear in the FrontPage Editor.

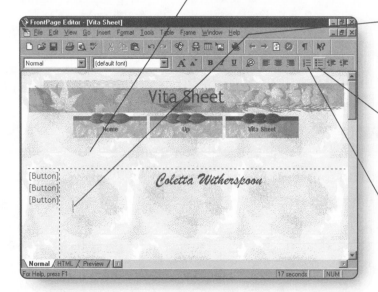

2. Click on the **place** where you want the list to begin. The insertion point will appear in the selected area.

3. Click on the **Bulleted List button**. A bullet will appear before the insertion point.

> ### NOTE
> If you want to create a numbered list, click on the Numbered List button.

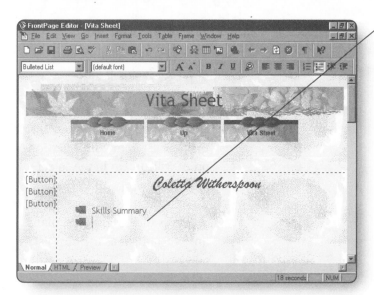

4. Type a **list item** and **press** the **Enter key**. The insertion point will move to the next line and another bullet will appear.

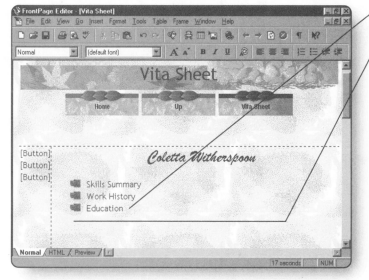

5. Type the rest of the **list items**.

6. Press the **Enter key twice** at the end of the last list item.

TIP

To convert normal text to a list, select the paragraphs that you want formatted as a list and click on the Bulleted List or Numbered list button.

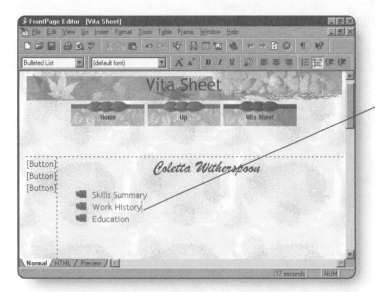

Inserting an Item in an Existing List

1. Click on the **end** of the line above where you want to place the new list item. The insertion point will appear in the selected place.

2. Press the **Enter key**. A blank line will appear as the next list entry.

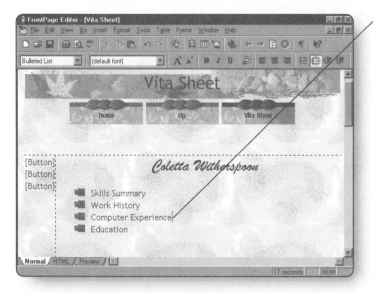

3. Type the new list **item** in this blank line. Do not press Enter unless you want to add another list item under this list item.

Adding Nested Items to the List

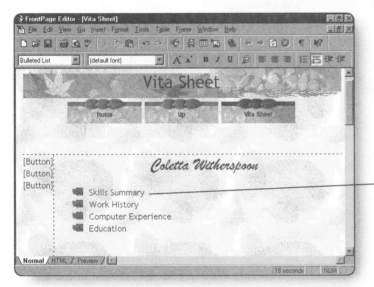

You can create sub-categories within your list if it needs to be in an outline format. These sub-categories are called nested items, and are indented from the main list. These sub-categories also use a different numbering scheme than your main list.

1. Click on the **end of the line** above where you want to start the nested list. The insertion point will appear in the selected place.

2. Press the **Enter key**. A blank line will appear.

3. Click on the **Increase Indent button**. The insertion point will move to the right.

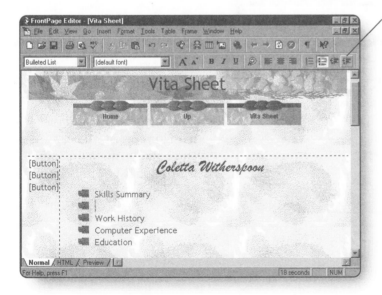

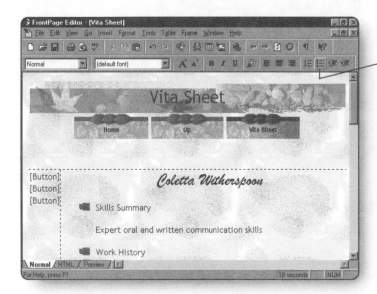

4. Type a list **item**.

5. **Click** on the **Bulleted List button**. The item will appear as a nested item.

6. **Press** the **Enter key**. The insertion point will move to the next line and another bullet will appear.

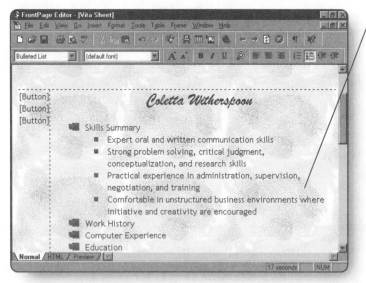

7. Type the rest of the list **items**.

TIP

If a nested item is the last item in your list, you can end both the main list and the nested list by pressing Ctrl+Enter.

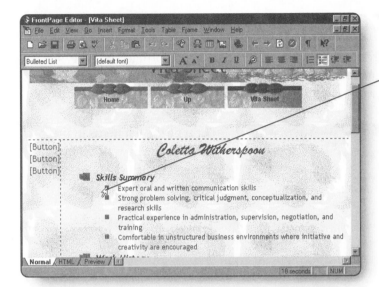

Deleting an Item from the List

1. Place the **mouse pointer** over the bullet that precedes the item you want to delete.

2. **Double-click** on the **bullet**. The item will be selected.

3. Click on the **Cut button**. The item will be deleted.

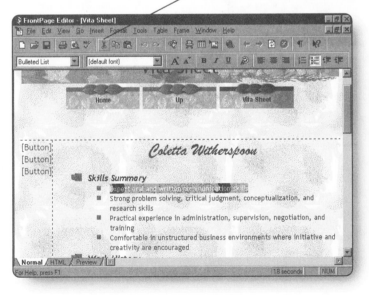

CREATING AN ORDERED LIST

Ordered lists are just as easy to build, format, and edit as bulleted lists. FrontPage gives you a little more control as to how these lists can be organized.

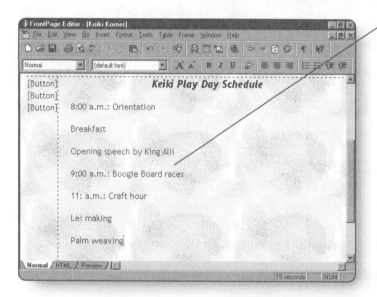

1. Type the list items in the order that you want them to appear in the list.

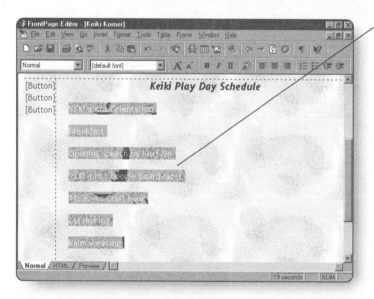

2. Select the entire list. The list will be highlighted.

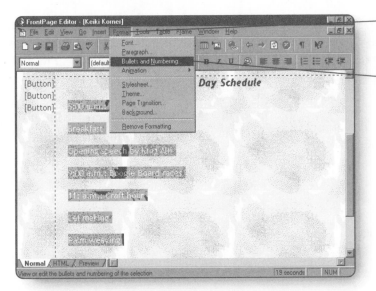

3. **Click** on **Format**. The Format menu will appear.

4. **Click** on **Bullets and Numbering**. The Bullets and Numbering dialog box will appear with the Image Bullets tab displayed.

5. **Click** on the **Numbers tab**. The Numbers tab will appear.

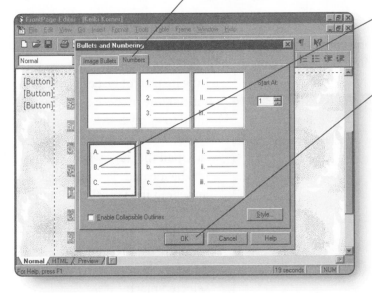

6. **Click** on the numbering **style** that you want to use. The style will be selected.

7. **Click** on **OK**. The list will be numbered according to the style you chose.

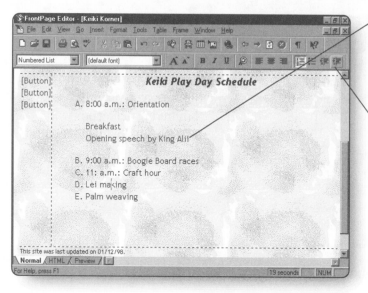

8. Click on the **items** that you want nested in the list. The insertion point will appear in that item.

9. Click on the **Increase Indent button**. The items will be indented.

USING STYLES TO FORMAT LISTS

There are other types of lists that you can create in FrontPage along with bulleted and numbered lists. These lists, called definition lists, usually contain list items that are a paragraph long instead of just one line. To format one of these lists, you will need to apply a style to the list.

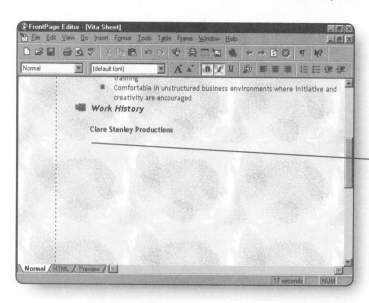

1. Open the **page** where the list will be located. The page will appear in the FrontPage Editor.

2. Click on the **place** where you want the list to begin. The pointer will appear in the selected place.

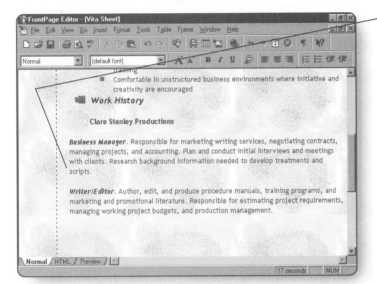

3. Type the list items.

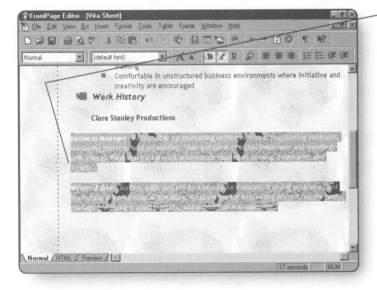

4. Select the list items to be formatted. The items will be highlighted.

5. **Click** on the **down arrow** to the right of the Change Style field. A drop-down list of styles will appear.

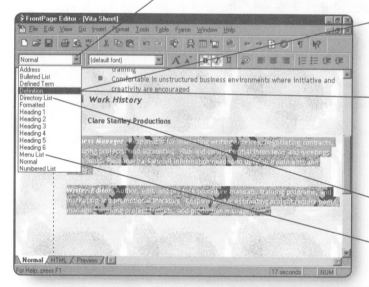

6. **Click** on the **style** you want to apply to the list items. The style will be applied.

✦ **Definition**. Definition lists include a term and its definition. The defined term appears against the left margin and the definition is indented.

✦ **Directory List**. A Directory List is a sequence of short terms.

✦ **Menu List**. A Menu List contains an unordered list of short entries.

BUILDING COLLAPSIBLE LISTS

Building a list that expands and collapses when a visitor clicks on an item used to require knowledge of Java or ActiveX. With the introduction of Dynamic HTML and the new collapsible list feature found in FrontPage 98, no special programming skills are necessary to create these lists.

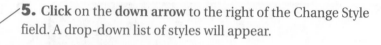

1. **Open** the **page** that contains the list you want to make into a collapsible outline. The page will appear in the FrontPage Editor.

2. **Type** and **format** the **list items**. You can use any of the list formats discussed earlier in this chapter to format the list items.

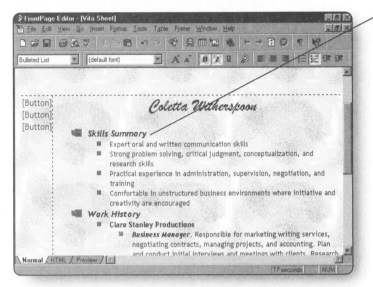

3. Click on the **list item** to which you want the collapsible outline feature enabled. Only those items that are nested in the list under this item will be collapsible. The level will be selected.

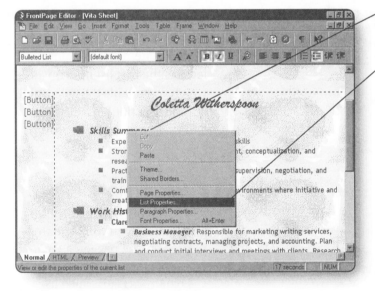

4. **Right-click** on the **item**. A shortcut menu will appear.

5. Click on **List Properties**. The List Properties dialog box will appear.

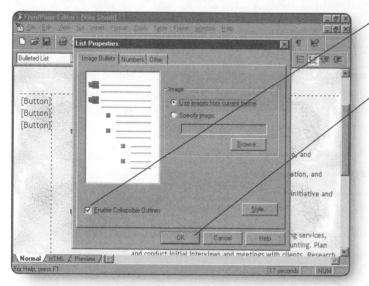

6. **Click** on **Enable Collapsible Outlines**. A check mark will appear in the box.

7. **Click** on **OK**. The collapsible outline feature for that level will be applied.

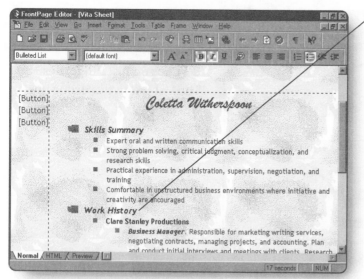

8. **Enable** the **collapsible outline** feature to the remainder of the list items (at the same level as the first list item on which you enable the collapsible outline function) in the list.

NOTE

To see your collapsible list in action, you will need to preview the page in a Web browser that supports Dynamic HTML, such as Microsoft Internet Explorer 4.0.

ADDING GRAPHICAL BULLETS

If you created your web using one of the FrontPage themes, you will notice that all of the bullet lists that you format contain graphical bullets. FrontPage does not limit you to these graphical bullets. You can change the graphical image used for bullets.

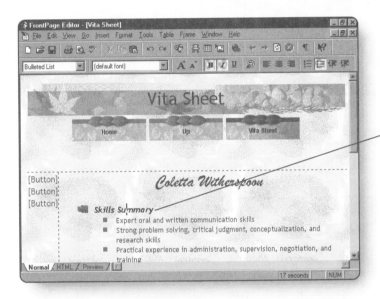

1. Open the **page** that contains the bulleted list to which you want to change the graphical bullets. The **page** will appear in the FrontPage Editor.

2. Click on the list **item** that contains the bullet to be changed. The item will be selected.

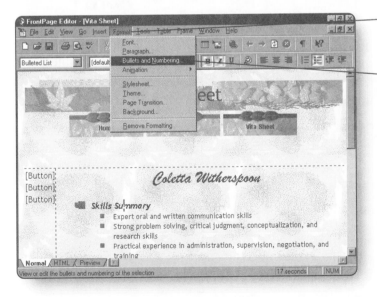

3. Click on **Format**. The Format menu will appear.

4. Click on **Bullets and Numbering**. The List Properties dialog box will appear with the Image Bullets tab displayed.

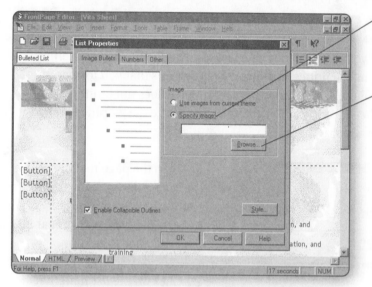

5. Click on the **Specify image option button**. The option will be selected.

6. Click on **Browse**. The Select image dialog box will appear.

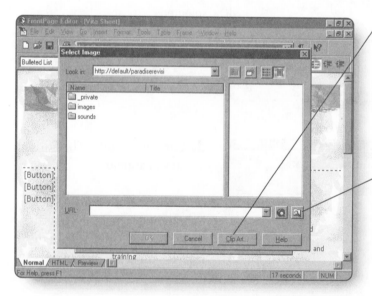

7. Click on **Clip Art**. The Microsoft Clip Gallery dialog box will appear.

NOTE

If you have an image stored on your computer that you want to use as a graphical bullet, click on the Select a File on Your Computer button.

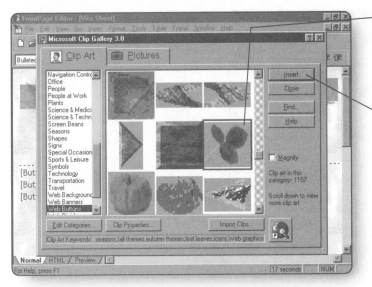

8. Select the **clip art** that you want to use as the bullet. The clip art image will be highlighted.

9. Click on **Insert**. The List Properties dialog box will appear and the path to the image will be displayed in the Specify image: text box.

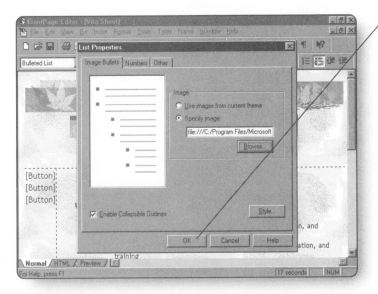

10. Click on **OK**. The bullet will be changed to the new bullet you selected.

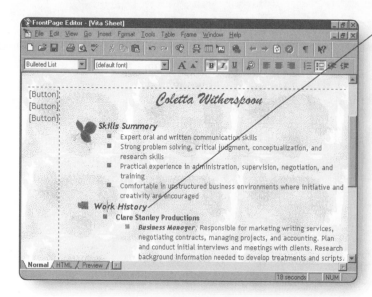

11. Change the remaining bullet **items** in the list.

7 Creating and Formatting Tables

You've probably seen tables used in spreadsheets and word processing documents. Tables are a great way to organize information. Tables are especially important in Web pages. Because you can't use the Tab key to create orderly columns of information, the best way to get around this obstacle is to use a table. Tables are also useful when you want to place text and graphics side by side. In this chapter, you'll learn how to:

✦ Create a simple table

✦ Add, delete, and merge rows and columns in a table

✦ Add text, images, and backgrounds to a table

CREATING A TABLE

Before you begin building tables, you may want to display the Table toolbar. The Table toolbar will help you build and edit tables quickly and efficiently.

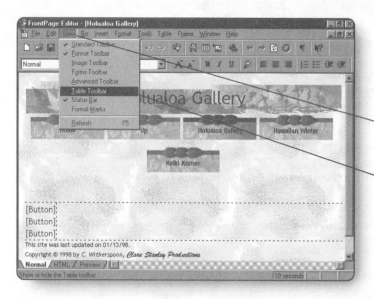

1. Open the **page** on which you want to create a table. The page will appear in the FrontPage Editor.

2. Click on **View**. The View menu will appear.

3. Click on **Table Toolbar**. The Table toolbar will appear below the other toolbars on the FrontPage Editor window.

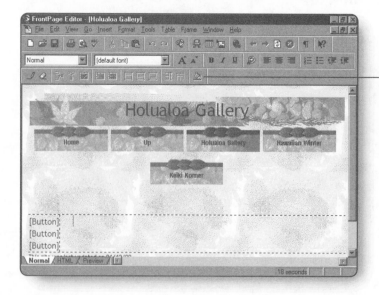

NOTE

The buttons on the Table toolbar are dimmed if the insertion point is not located inside a table.

Creating the Border

Before you begin building your table, you should have an approximate idea of the size of the table you want. If you aren't exactly sure, don't fret. You can always add and delete rows and columns later.

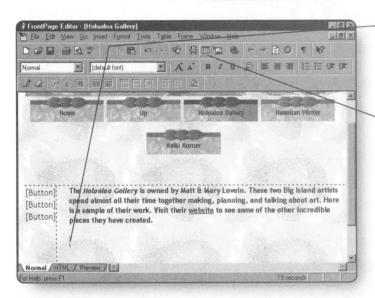

1. **Click** on the **place** where you want to insert the table. The insertion point will appear in the selected position.

2. **Click** on the **Insert Table button**. A table palette will appear.

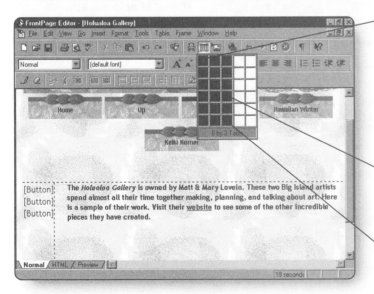

3. **Click** and **hold** the **mouse button** on the upper-left cell of the table palette. The table size will appear at the bottom of the table palette showing you the number of rows and columns that will be created.

4. **Drag** the **mouse pointer** down and to the right. The table size will grow.

5. **Release** the **mouse button** when the table is the desired size. A blank table will appear on the page.

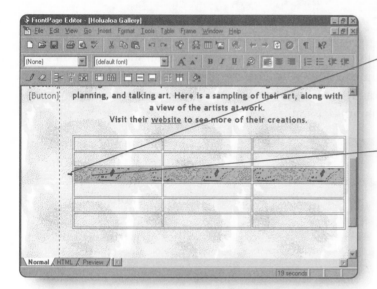

Adding Rows

1. **Place** the **mouse pointer** along the left edge of the table. The mouse pointer will change to a right pointing arrow.

2. **Click** on the **row** that you want to be below the new row. The row will be selected.

TIP

To add multiple rows at one time, select several rows. The same number of rows will be inserted into the table.

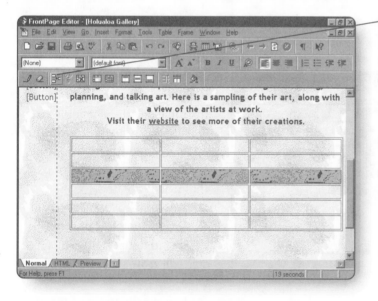

3. **Click** on the **Insert Rows button**. A new row will be added to the table and will appear above the selected row.

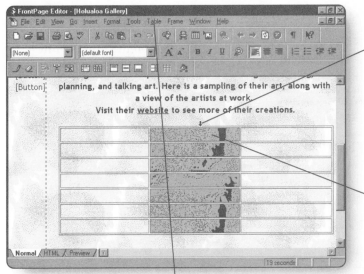

Adding Columns

1. **Place** the **mouse pointer** along the top edge of the table so that it is above the column to the right of the position where you want to place the new column. The mouse pointer will change to an arrow.

2. **Click** on the **column** that you want to be on the right side of the new column. The column will be selected.

NOTE

The Insert Rows or Columns command on the Table menu gives you more control when adding rows and columns.

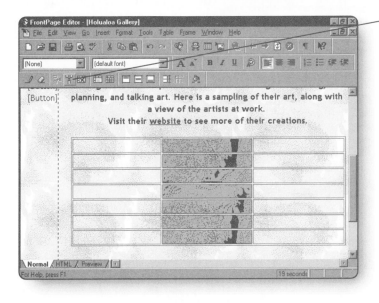

3. **Click** on the **Insert Columns button**. A new column will be added to the table and will appear to the left of the selected column.

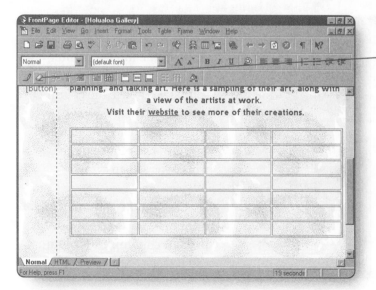

Merging Cells

1. **Click** on the **Eraser button**. The mouse pointer will turn into an eraser.

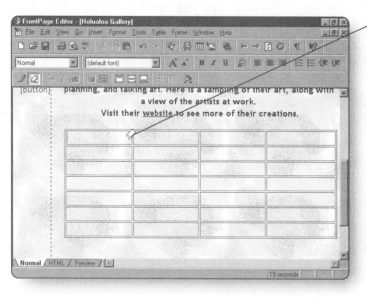

2. **Click** and **hold** the **mouse button** on the left side of the cell border between the two cells that you want to merge in the row.

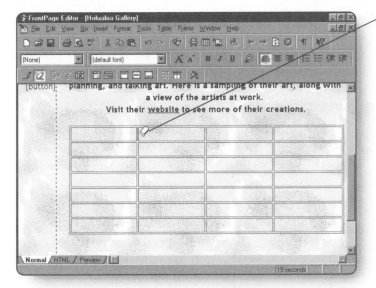

3. **Drag** the **mouse pointer** to the right across the cell border. The cell border will be selected.

4. **Release** the **mouse button**. The two cells will be merged.

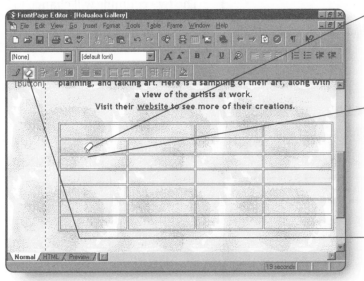

5. **Click** and **hold** the **mouse button** above the cell border between the two cells that you want to merge in the column.

6. **Drag** the **mouse pointer** down across the cell border. The cell border will be selected. When you release the mouse button, the two cells will be merged.

7. **Click** on the **Eraser button**. The merge function will be turned off.

Changing the Column Width

You'll notice that the columns in your table are an equal width. You can change the width of columns to fit your needs.

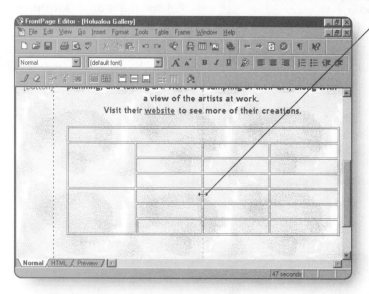

1. **Position** the **mouse pointer** on the line between the two columns you want to change. The mouse pointer will turn into two arrowheads.

2. **Press** and **hold** the **mouse button** and **drag** the line to the **left** or to the **right** to change the size of the columns.

3. **Release** the **mouse button**. The two columns will change to different widths.

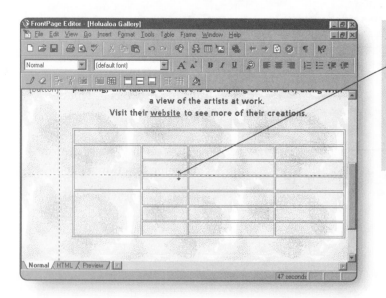

TIP

You can change the row height by positioning the mouse pointer on a line and holding the mouse button while dragging up or down.

Using the Drawing Tools to Add Cells

You can easily add a new cell or additional rows and columns to your table.

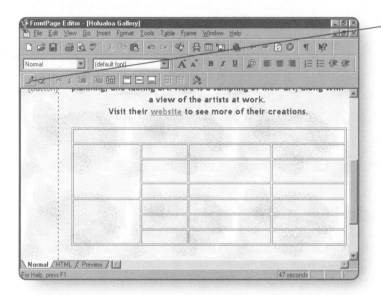

1. **Click** on the **Draw Table button**. The mouse pointer will turn into a pencil.

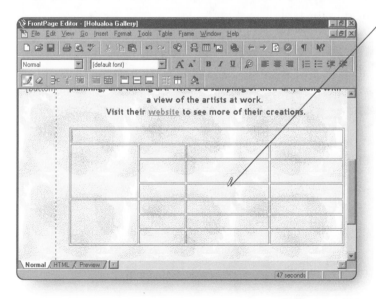

2. **Press** and **hold** the **mouse button** on the location where you want to start the new cell.

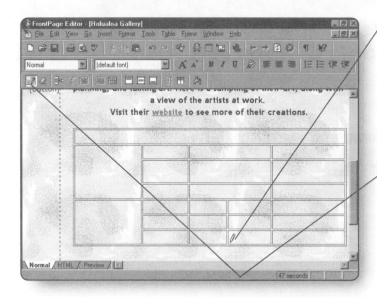

3. Drag the **mouse pointer** to the location where you want to end the new cell.

4. Release the **mouse button**. A new cell or group of cells will be added to the table.

5. Click on the **Draw Table button**. The drawing feature will be turned off.

Adding a Caption

If you want to leave your visitors a message about the contents of the table, add a caption.

1. Click **anywhere** inside the table. The insertion bar will appear in the table.

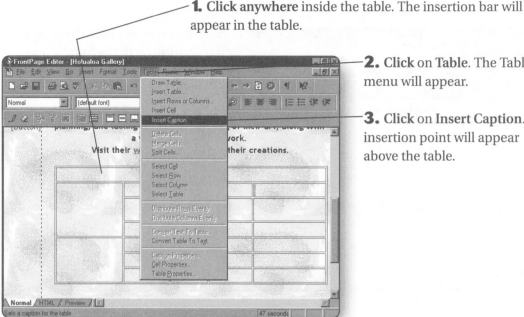

2. Click on **Table**. The Table menu will appear.

3. Click on **Insert Caption**. The insertion point will appear above the table.

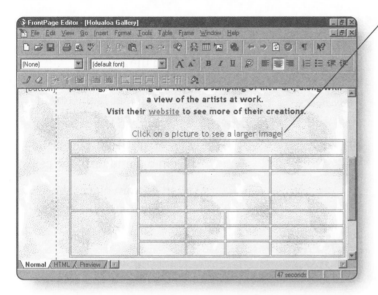

4. Type a **caption** for the table.

5. Click on a **blank area** on the page. The caption will be created above the table.

INSERTING CONTENT INTO A CELL

After you have built a structure for your table, you can begin to add some words and pictures.

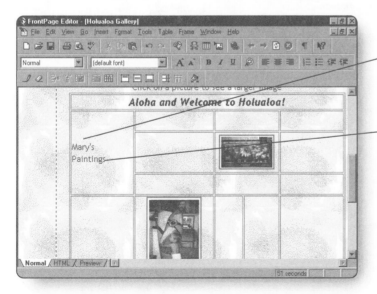

Adding Text

1. Click in the **cell** where you want to place the text. The insertion bar will appear in the cell.

2. Type the **text**.

TIP

To add a second row of text, press the Enter key for a separate paragraph or press Shift+Enter to keep the lines within a single paragraph.

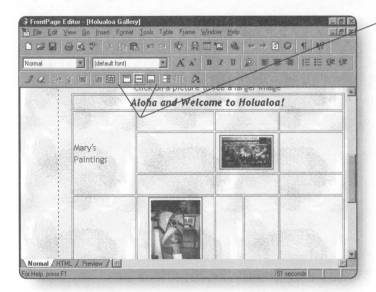

3. **Click** on a **paragraph position button**. The text will be aligned in the cell.

✦ **Align Top** places the text at the top of the cell.

✦ **Center Vertically** places the text in the middle of the cell.

✦ **Align Bottom** places the text at the bottom of the cell.

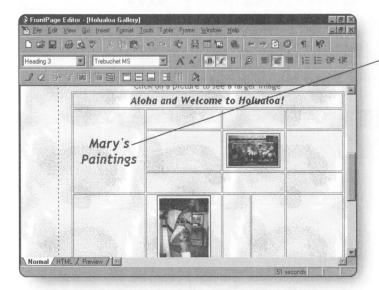

NOTE

You can format text the same way you would in any other place on a Web page. You can use the formatting toolbar, the style list, or the format menu commands.

Adding Images

1. Click in the **cell** where you want to place the image. The insertion bar will appear in the cell.

2. Click on **Insert**. The Insert menu will appear.

3. Click on **Clipart**. The Microsoft Clip Art Gallery dialog box will appear.

4. Click on the clip art **image** that you want to insert into the table. The image will be selected.

5. Click on **Insert**. The image will appear in the cell.

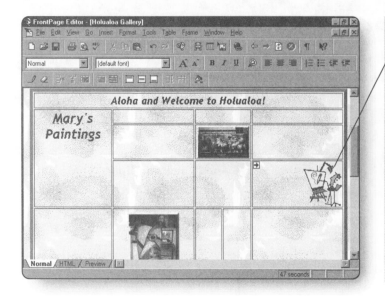

TIP

You can change the size of the inserted image by clicking on it to display the image handles. Then click and hold an image handle while you move the mouse pointer away from the image to make it larger or toward the image to make it smaller. To learn more about working with images in your web, see Chapter 8, "Working with Image Tools."

DETAILING A TABLE

After you have created a table and added some text and graphics, you may decide that the table lacks color. You can spruce up your tables by adding background colors and images and by changing the color of the border lines.

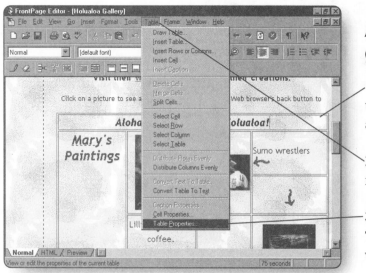

Adding a Background to a Table

1. Click anywhere inside the table. The insertion bar will appear in the table.

2. Click on Table. The Table menu will appear.

3. Click on Table Properties. The Table Properties dialog box will appear.

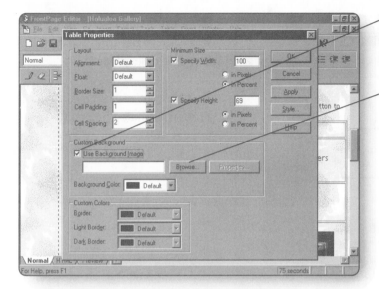

4. **Click** on **Use Background Image**. A check mark will appear in the box.

5. **Click** on the **Browse button**. The Select Background Image dialog box will appear.

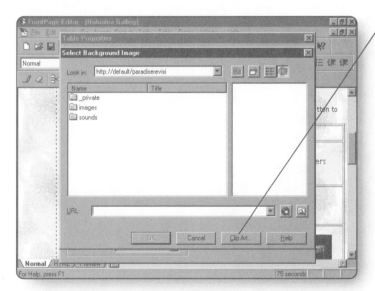

6. **Click** on the **Clip Art button**. The Microsoft Clip Gallery will appear.

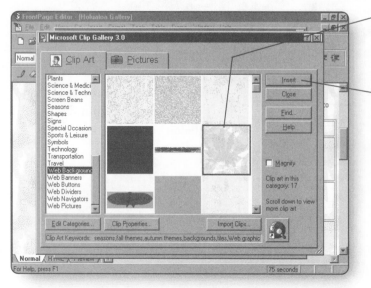

7. **Click** on a **background** that you want to use in the table. The image will be selected.

8. **Click** on **Insert**. The Table Properties dialog box will appear.

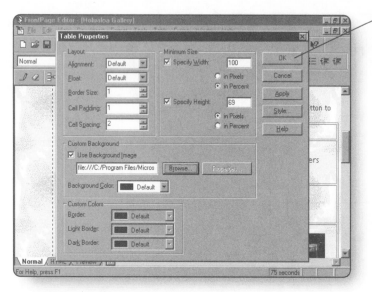

9. **Click** on **OK**. The background image will be applied to the table.

Changing the Color of a Cell

1. **Click** on the **cell** in which you want to change the background color. The insertion bar will appear in the cell.

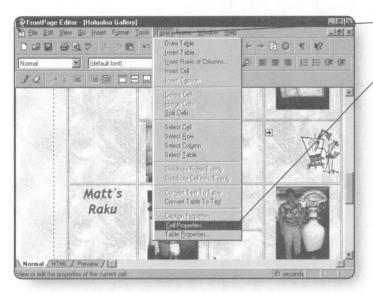

2. **Click** on **Table**. The Table menu will appear.

3. **Click** on **Cell Properties**. The Cell Properties dialog box will appear.

4. **Click** and **hold** on the **down arrow** on the Background color drop-down list. A list of available colors will appear.

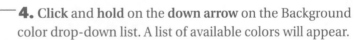

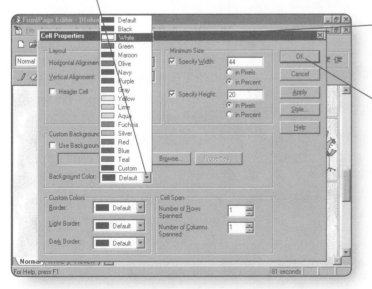

5. **Drag** the **mouse pointer** over a color. The color will be selected.

6. **Click** on **OK**. The color will be applied to the background for the selected cell.

Coloring Table Borders

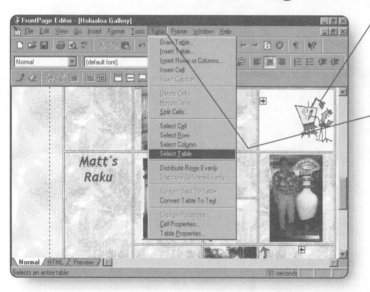

1. **Click** inside the **table** in a cell where you want to change the border color. The insertion bar will appear in the selected cell.

2. **Click** on **Table**. The Table menu will appear.

3. **Select** one of the following **command**s:

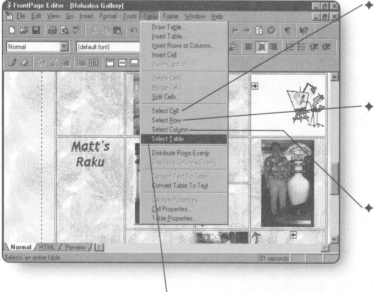

✦ **Select Cell** highlights the cell where the insertion point is placed. You will only be able to change the border colors for this cell.

✦ **Select Row** highlights the row where the insertion point is placed. You will only be able to change the border colors for this row.

✦ **Select Column** highlights the column where the insertion point is placed. You will only be able to change the border colors for this column.

✦ **Select Table** highlights the entire table. You will be able to change the border colors for the entire table.

4. Click on **Table**. The Table menu will appear.

5. Click on **Cell Properties**. The Cell Properties dialog box will appear.

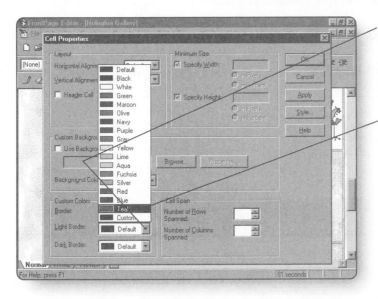

6. Click on the **down arrow** next to the Light Border: drop-down list. A list of colors will appear.

7. Click on a **color**. The color will be selected.

8. **Click** on the **down arrow** next to the Dark Border: drop-down list. A list of colors will appear.

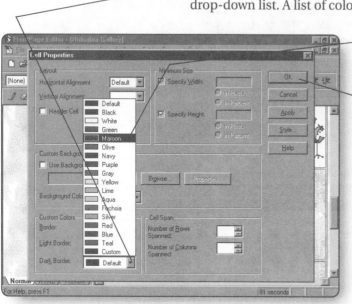

9. **Click** on a **color**. The color will be selected.

10. **Click** on OK. The new border colors will be applied to the table.

CONVERTING TEXT INTO A TABLE

You can type the information that you want to appear in a table before you build the table. By doing this, FrontPage will automatically format the table to fit the text.

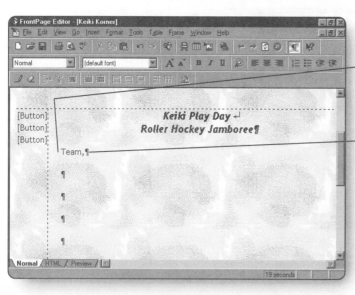

1. **Click** on the **place** where you want to start the table. The insertion bar will appear.

2. **Type** the **text** (followed by a comma) that you want to appear in the first column of the first row.

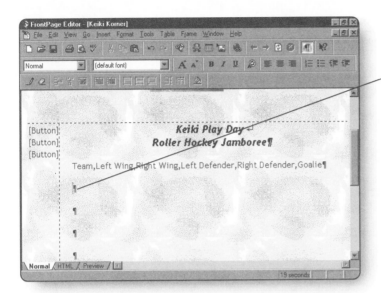

3. **Type** additional row **entries** followed by a comma.

4. **Type** the last row **entry** and **press** the **Enter key**. The insertion bar will appear on the next line.

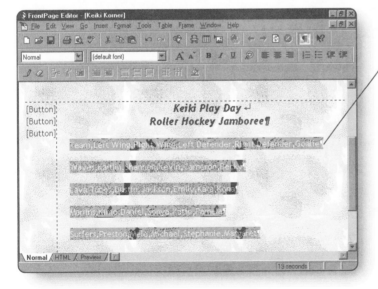

5. **Add** additional **rows** to the table as needed.

6. **Select** the **text** that you want to convert to a table. The text will be selected.

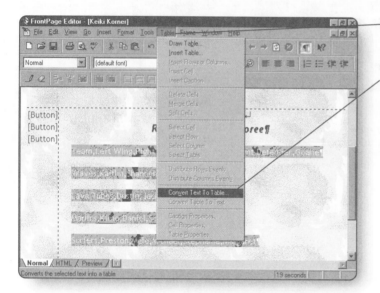

7. Click on **Table**. The Table menu will appear.

8. Click on **Convert Text To Table**. The Convert Text To Table dialog box will appear.

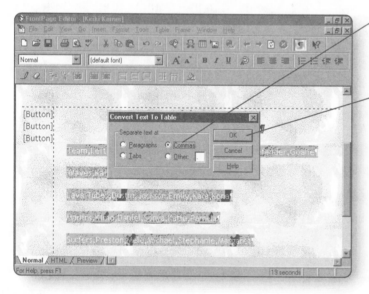

9. Click on the **Commas option**. The option will be selected.

10. Click on **OK**. The text will appear inside a table.

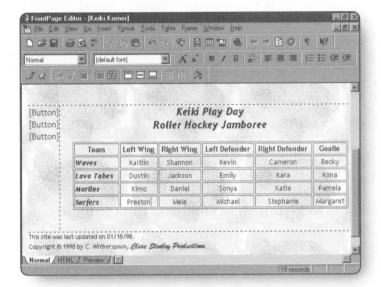

11. Format the **text** and the **table** to make it more appealing.

PART II REVIEW QUESTIONS

1. Can you use more than one theme in a web? *See "Applying a Theme to an Individual Web Page" in Chapter 5.*

2. How many border frames can you display in your Web pages? *See "Setting Border Frames" in Chapter 5.*

3. Which navigation option allows visitors to your site to flip through pages on the same level? *See "Applying Navigation Buttons" in Chapter 5.*

4. What are the events that can be associated with a page transition? *See "Adding Page Transitions" in Chapter 5.*

5. What are the two types of simple lists that you can create on your Web pages? *See "Creating Simple Lists" in Chapter 6.*

6. Besides using toolbar buttons to format a list, what is the other method you can use? *See "Using Styles to Format Lists" in Chapter 6.*

7. How can you use your own graphics as bullets instead of using the default bullets used by FrontPage? *See "Adding Graphical Bullets" in Chapter 6.*

8. If you don't want to use the menu to create a table, where do you find toolbar buttons that you can use to create and edit a table? *See "Building the Table" in Chapter 7.*

9. How can you add several rows to a table in one quick and easy step? *See "Adding Rows" in Chapter 7.*

10. If you have text on a Web page, how can you convert this text into a table? *See "Converting Text into a Table" in Chapter 7.*

PART III
Enhancing Your Web

gif
a.jpg
ey.gif
a.jpg
ntpag.gif
ish.jpg
respond.gif
shark.gif
sunset.gif

URL: image

HTML / Preview /

8 Working with Image Tools

Pictures are common on Web pages. Most of the pictures that you can add to your pages will be of two types: JPEG and GIF. JPEG images include high color pictures, such as scanned images of photographs. GIFs are pictures that are created in a computer drawing program and use only a few colors. GIF images can be stationary or animated. Pictures can do a lot to enhance your web, but make sure they are appropriate to the message that you want to convey to your visitors. In this chapter, you'll learn how to:

✦ Display images on your Web pages

✦ Add images to the Microsoft Clip Gallery

✦ Edit and enhance your images

INSERTING IMAGES

There are a number of places where you can find artwork to place on your Web pages. The easiest place to find pictures is with the Clip Art Gallery provided by Microsoft. If you've had a chance to play with any of the graphics software programs, you may have created pictures that can be used in your web.

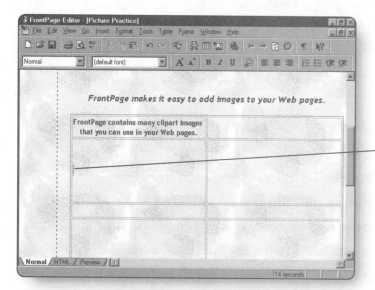

Finding Clip Art

1. Open the **page** where you want to insert the clip art image. The page will appear in the FrontPage Editor.

2. Click in the **place** where you want to insert the image. The insertion bar will appear in the selected place.

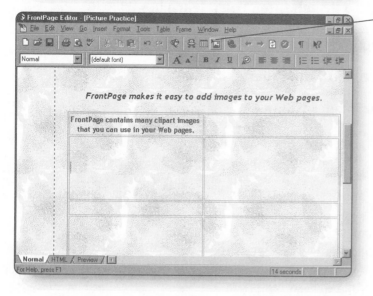

3. Click on the **Insert Image button**. The Image dialog box will appear.

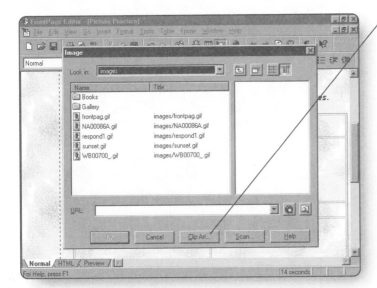

4. Click on the **Clip Art button**. The Microsoft Clip Gallery will appear.

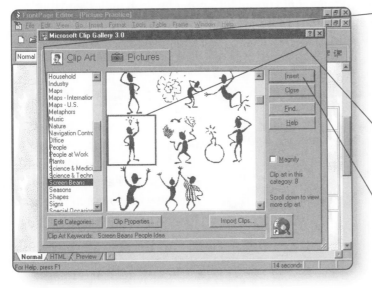

5. Click on a **category** of clip art that matches the type of image you want to add to your Web page. The category will be selected.

6. Click on the **image** that you want to add to the Web page. The image will be selected.

7. Click on **Insert**. The image will appear on the Web page.

8. Click on the **image**. The image will be selected.

9. Click and **hold** one of the corner **image handles,** and then **drag** the **mouse pointer** toward the image to make it smaller or away from the image to make it larger. The image will be resized.

Adding Images to the Clip Gallery

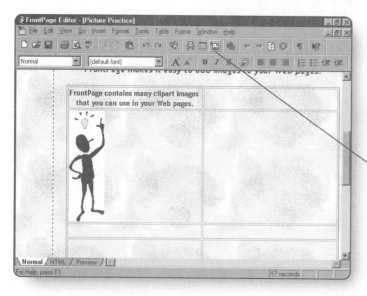

Several Microsoft programs, such as those in Microsoft Office, use the Microsoft Clip Gallery. If you have an image that you want to use in your Web pages or other programs, you can add it to the Clip Gallery.

1. Click on the **Insert Image button**. The Image dialog box will appear.

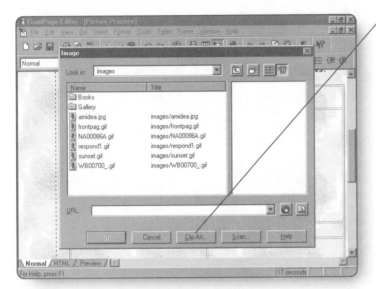

2. Click on the **Clip Art button**. The Microsoft Image Gallery will appear.

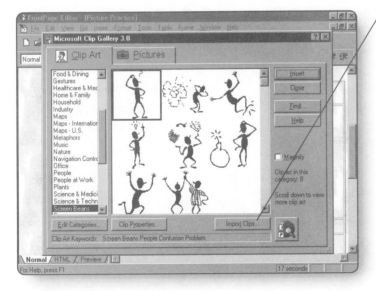

3. Click on the **Import Clips button**. The Add clip art to Clip Gallery dialog box will appear.

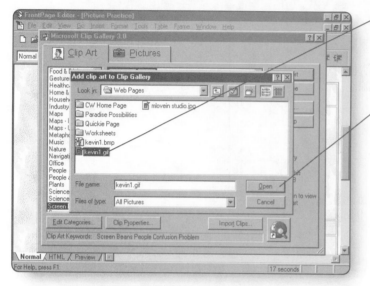

4. **Click** on the **image file** that you want to add to the Clip Gallery. The image will be selected.

5. **Click** on **Open**. The Clip Properties dialog box will appear.

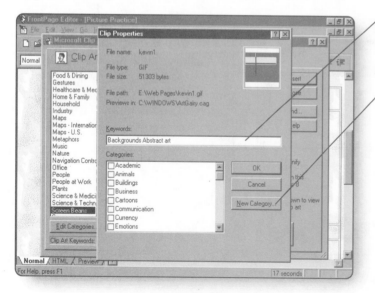

6. **Type keywords** that describe the image you are adding to the Clip Gallery.

7. **Click** on the **New Category button**. The New Category dialog box will appear.

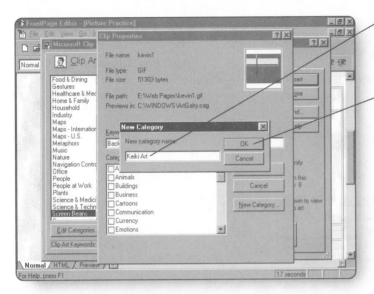

8. **Type** a **title** in the New category name: text box. The title will be entered.

9. **Click** on **OK**. The new category will appear in the Category list of the Clip Properties dialog box and will be selected.

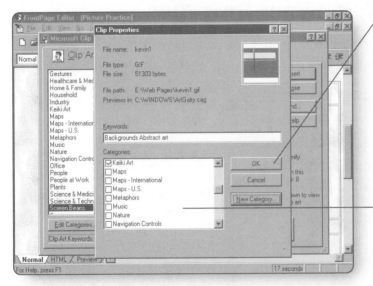

10. **Click** on **OK**. The Clip Properties dialog box will close and the Image dialog box will appear.

TIP

You may need to browse through the list of categories and make sure that no other categories are checked. If other categories are checked, the image will be added to all the selected categories.

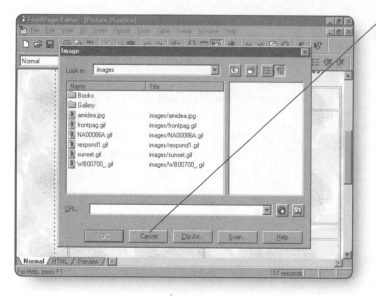

11. **Click** on **Cancel**. The image will be added to the Clip Gallery without inserting an image onto the Web page.

Using Your Own Files

You may have an image on your computer that you wish to put on your Web page.

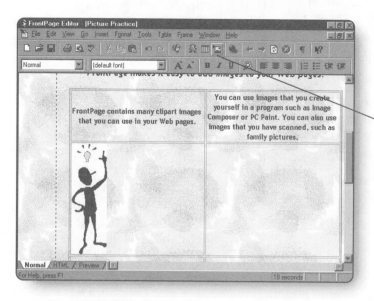

1. **Click** on the **place** where you want to insert the image. The insertion bar will appear in the selected position.

2. **Click** on the **Insert Image button**. The Image dialog box will appear.

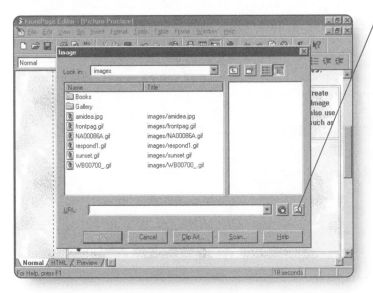

3. Click on the **Select a file on your computer button**. The Select File dialog box will appear.

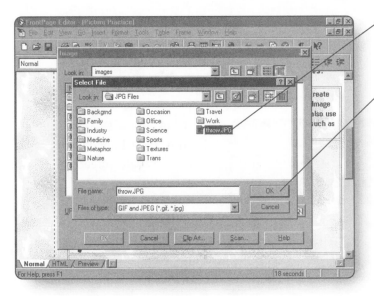

4. Click on the **file** that you want to insert. The image file will be selected.

5. Click on **OK**. The image will be inserted on the Web page.

Saving Images to FrontPage

After you have added an image to a Web page, you will need to save the page. When you do this, FrontPage will ask you where you want the file saved.

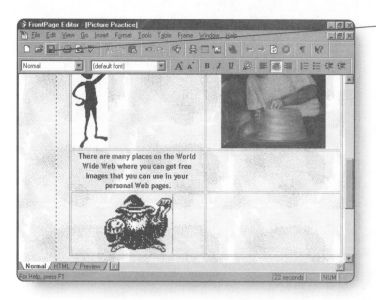

1. Click on the **Save button**. The Save Embedded Files dialog box will appear.

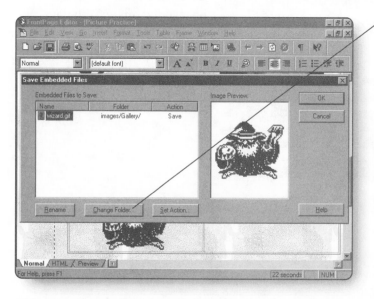

2. Click on the **Change Folder button**. The Change Folder dialog box will appear.

NOTE

You may want to store your images in a different folder than where your Web pages are stored. By doing this, you will be able to find image files easier. To learn more about managing files and folders in FrontPage, see Chapter 14 "Updating Your Web."

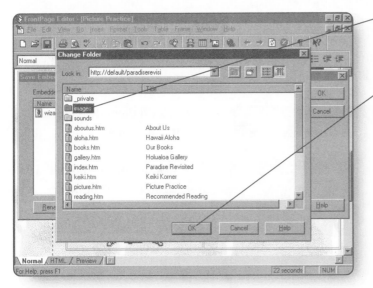

3. Click on the **folder** where you want to save the image file. The folder will be selected.

4. Click on **OK**. The Save Embedded Files dialog box will appear.

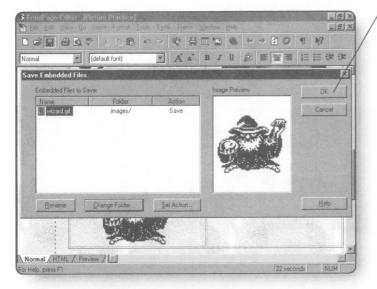

5. Click on **OK**. The image will be saved to your web.

EDITING IMAGES

The image editing tools that are available in the FrontPage Editor appear on the Image toolbar.

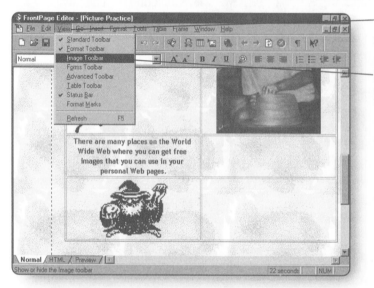

1. Click on **View**. The View menu will appear.

2. Click on **Image Toolbar**. The Image toolbar will appear.

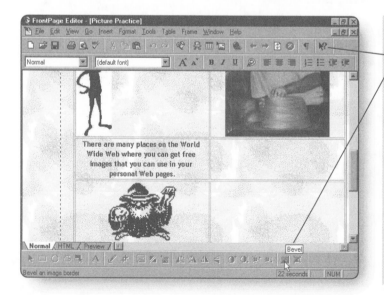

Making Images Look Washed Out

The Washout command creates a light-colored (almost transparent) version of an image. This command is useful if you don't want an image to stand out on a page or if you want to place text over an image so that the text is readable.

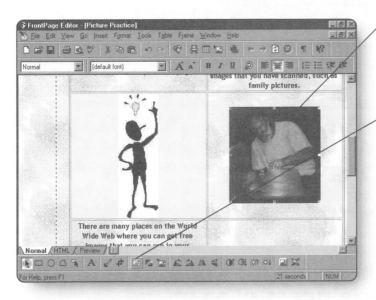

1. Click on the **image** to which you want to apply the washout effect. The image will be selected.

2. Click on the **Washout button** on the Image Toolbar. The image will appear in paler colors.

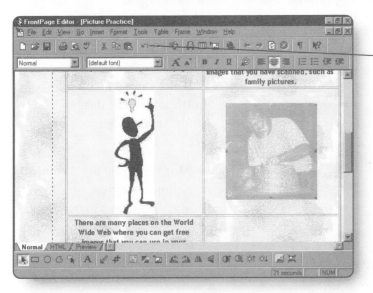

TIP

If you do not like the effect you applied, click on the Undo button on the Standard toolbar. The image will revert back to the last saved image.

Turning Color Pictures Black and White

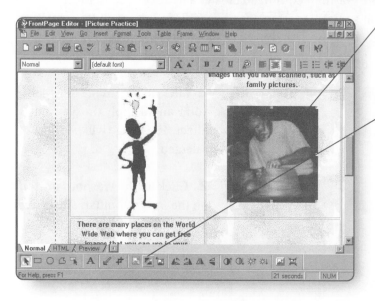

1. Click on the **color image** that you want to change to black and white. The image will be selected.

2. Click on the **Black and White button**. The image will look like a black and white photograph.

Changing the Contrast and Brightness of an Image

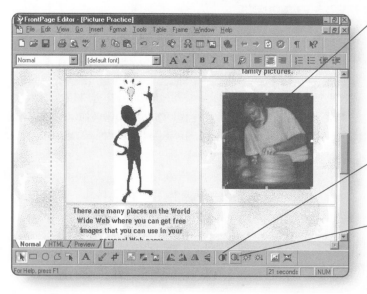

1. Click on the **image**. The image will be selected.

2. Click on the following **buttons** until the desired contrast and brightness are achieved:

✦ **More Contrast** to add more definition between the light and dark colors in the image.

✦ **Less Contrast** to soften images that are too harsh.

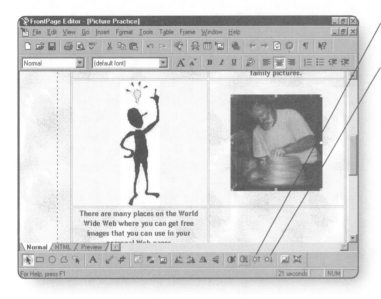

✦ **More Brightness** to increase the lightness of the image.

✦ **Less Brightness** to decrease the lightness of the image.

NOTE

Unlike other buttons on the Image toolbar, the brightness and contrast buttons can be clicked more than once to achieve the desired effect in different degrees.

Adding a Bevel Edge to an Image

You may wish to place a frame around your images.

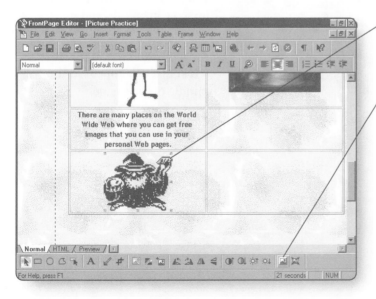

1. Click on the **image** to which you want to add a bevel edge. The image will be selected.

2. Click on the **Bevel button**. The bevel will be applied.

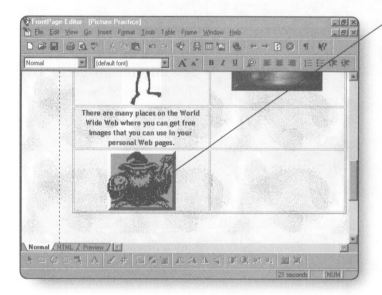

The image will appear framed.

Placing Text Over an Image

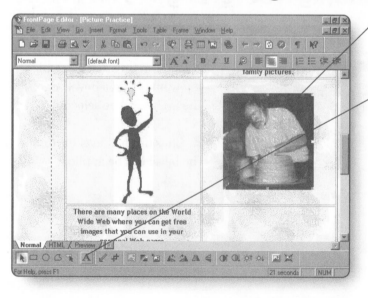

1. Click on the **image** to which you want to add the text. The image will be selected.

2. Click on the **Text button**. A text box will appear in the middle of the image.

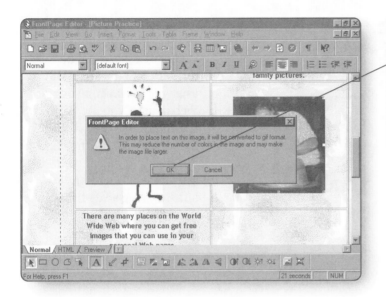

NOTE

If the image is not GIF in format, FrontPage will need to convert the image before you can proceed. Click on OK.

3. Type the **text**.

4. Click outside the text box when you are finished typing. The text will appear over the image.

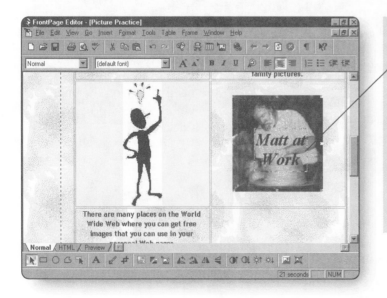

TIP

Text over images can be formatted in the same way as any other text on your Web page. If you increase the size of the font, you may have to make the text box larger by clicking on one of the border handles and dragging away from the text.

Cropping Images

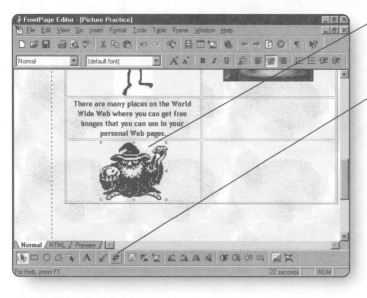

1. **Click** on the **image** that you want to crop. The image will be selected.

2. **Click** on the **Crop button**. A blue box with image handles will appear around the image.

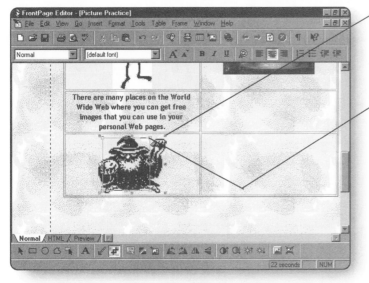

3. Place the **mouse pointer** over one of the image handles. The mouse pointer will turn into a vertical double arrow.

4. Click and **hold** an **image handle**, then **drag** the **mouse** toward the image. The crop marks will appear inside the image.

5. Release the **mouse button** when the undesired portion of the image is outside the crop marks.

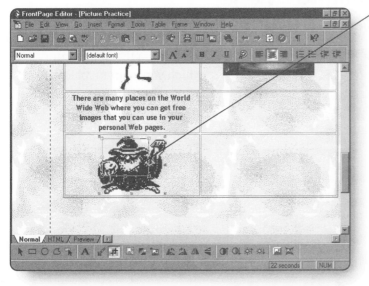

6. Move the **crop marks** on the other sides of the image as needed.

7. Press the **Enter key**. The cropped image will appear on the page.

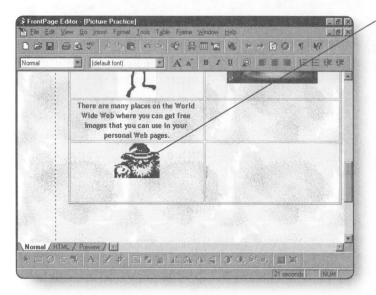

Only the desired portion of the image will remain on the Web page.

Making Image Backgrounds Transparent

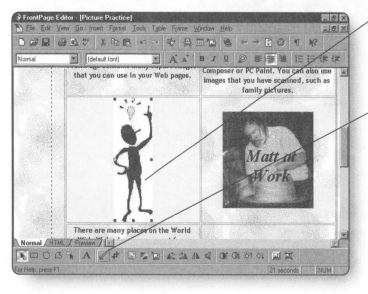

1. **Click** on the **image** from which you want to make the background disappear. The image will be selected.

2. **Click** on the **Transparent button**. The mouse pointer will turn into the eraser end of a pencil.

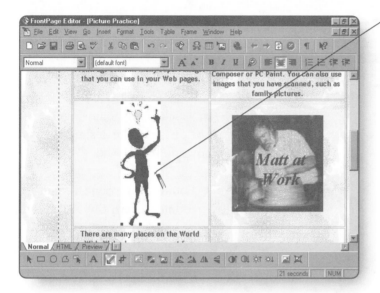

3. **Click** on the **background color** that you want to make disappear.

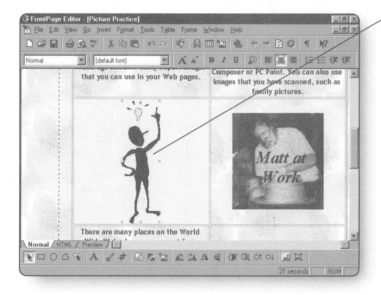

The image background will disappear and the background of the Web page will appear in place of the image background.

Rotating Images

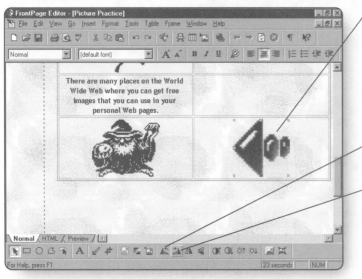

1. **Click** on the **image**. The image will be selected.

2. **Click** on the following **buttons** until the desired position is achieved:

✦ **Rotate Left** to rotate the image counterclockwise by 90 degrees.

✦ **Rotate Right** to rotate the image clockwise by 90 degrees.

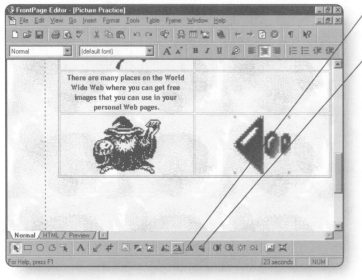

✦ **Reverse** to flip the image horizontally.

✦ **Flip** to flip the image vertically.

> ### NOTE
> The rotation buttons can be clicked until the desired position is achieved.

9 Creating Dynamic Effects

Well designed graphics can convey messages, but there may be times when you want your graphics to reach out and grab your audience. How can you convince your graphics to sing, dance, and perform? This has always been a relatively easy task for programmers. Now, if you lack programming skills, you can still make your graphics perform somersaults across the page using the built-in ActiveX and Java Controls in FrontPage. In this chapter, you'll learn how to:

✦ Build flashy hover buttons

✦ Create banners that flip and marquees that slide

✦ Count the number of people that have seen your performing graphics

USING HOVER BUTTONS

You may have noticed that some Web pages contain graphics that change their appearance when you place the mouse pointer over them. These graphics are called *hover buttons*.

Creating Standard Hover Buttons

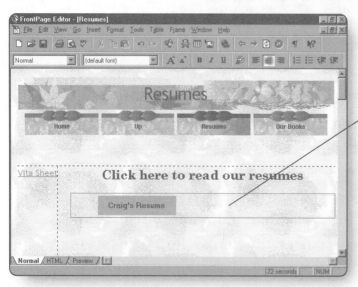

1. Open the **page** where you want the hover button to appear. The page will appear in the FrontPage Editor.

2. Click on the **place** where you want to position the hover button. The insertion bar will appear in the position.

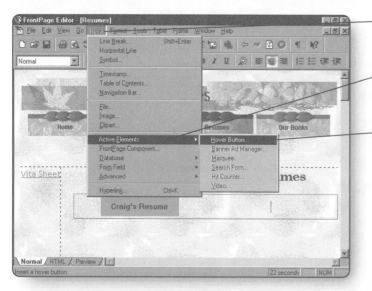

3. Click on **Insert**. The Insert menu will appear.

4. Click on **Active Elements**. A second menu will appear.

5. Click on **Hover Button**. The Hover Button dialog box will appear.

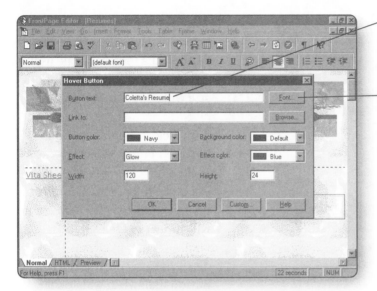

6. **Type** the **text** that you want to appear on the hover button in the Button text: text box.

7. **Click** on the **Font button**. The Font dialog box will appear.

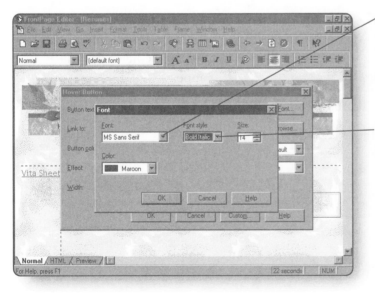

8. **Click** on the **down arrow** next to the Font: drop-down list and **select** a **font** to be used on the hover button. The font will appear in the list box.

9. **Click** on the **down arrow** next to the Font Style: drop-down list and **select** a **font style** to be used on the hover button. The font style will appear in the list box.

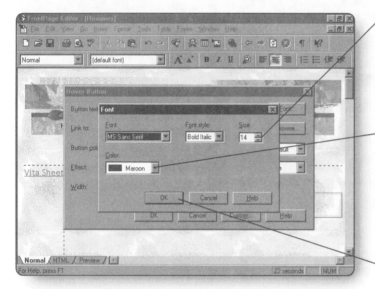

10. Click on the **up** and **down arrows** next to the Size: text box and select a font size to be used on the hover button. The font size will appear in the box.

11. Click and **hold** the **mouse button** on the down arrow next to the Color: drop-down list and select a font color to be used on the hover button. The font color will appear in the list box.

12. Click on **OK**. The Hover Button dialog box will appear.

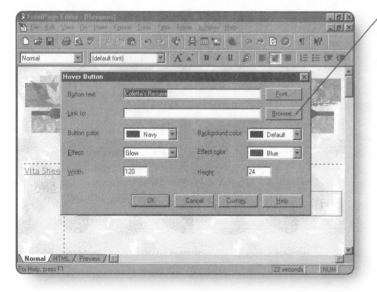

13. Click on the **Browse** button. The Select Hover Button Hyperlink dialog box will appear.

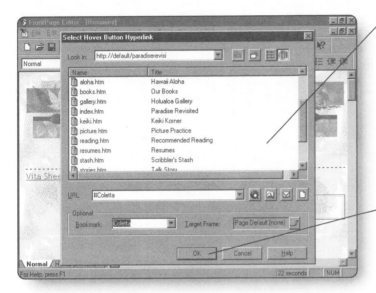

14. **Select** the **page** to which you want to create a hyperlink.

15. **Click** on **OK**. The Hover Button dialog box will appear.

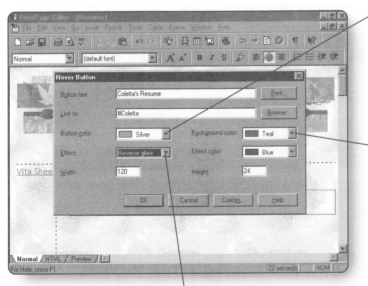

16. **Click** and **hold** the **down arrow** next to the Button color: list box and select a color to be used in the foreground of the hover button. The color will appear in the list box.

17. **Click** and **hold** the **down arrow** next to the Background color: list box and select a color to be used in the background of the hover button. The color will appear in the list box.

18. **Click** on the **down arrow** next to the Effect: list box and select an effect that will appear when your visitor places the mouse pointer over the hover button. The effect will appear in the list box.

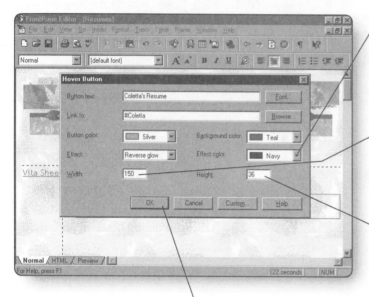

19. Click and **hold** the **down arrow** next to the Effect color: list box and select a color for the effect. The effect color will appear in the list box.

20. **Double-click** in the **Width: text box** and type the desired width of the hover button, in pixels.

21. **Double-click** in the **Height: text box** and type the desired height of the hover button, in pixels.

22. Click on **OK**. The hover button will be created.

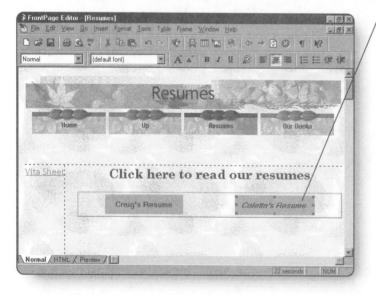

The hover button.

Editing Hover Buttons

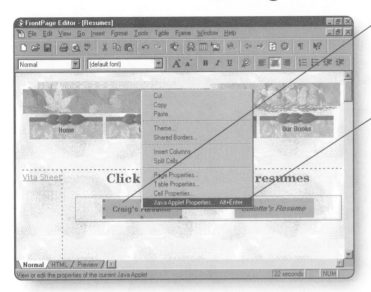

1. Right-click on the **hover button** to which you want to make changes. A shortcut menu will appear.

2. Click on **Java Applet Properties**. The Hover Button dialog box will appear.

3. Make the **changes** that you want to the hover button.

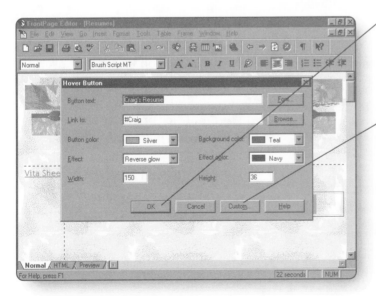

4. Click on **OK**. The changes will be applied.

TIP

To be creative, click on the Custom button. The resulting dialog box allows you to play a sound when the hover button is clicked. It also lets you use your own images as hover buttons. You can create your own images in a program such as Microsoft Image Composer, which comes bundled with FrontPage.

CREATING BANNERS

The Banner Ad Manager lets you take several images and display them in a slideshow fashion. The pictures flip from one to the next at a set interval. You can also add a transition effect between images, adding even more pizzazz.

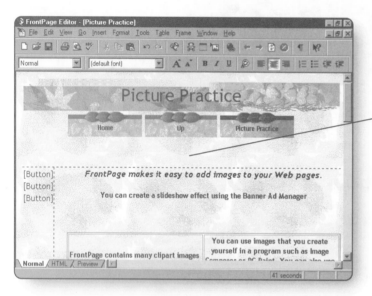

1. Open the **page** where you want to place the banner. The page will appear in the FrontPage Editor.

2. Click on the **place** where you want to position the banner. The insertion bar will appear in the selected position.

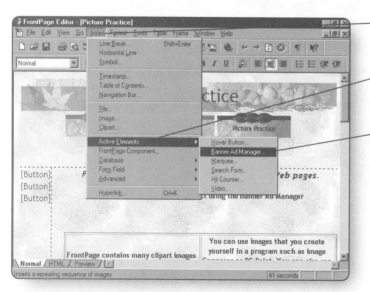

3. Click on **Insert**. The Insert menu will appear.

4. Click on **Active Elements**. A second menu will appear.

5. Click on **Banner Ad Manager**. The Banner Ad Manager dialog box will appear.

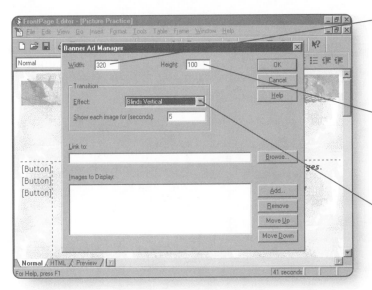

6. **Double-click** in the **Width: text box** and **type** the **number** of pixels wide you want the banner to be.

7. **Double-click** in the **Height: text box** and **type** the **number** of pixels high you want the banner to be.

8. **Click** on the **down arrow** to the right of the Effect: list box and select an effect for the transition between images.

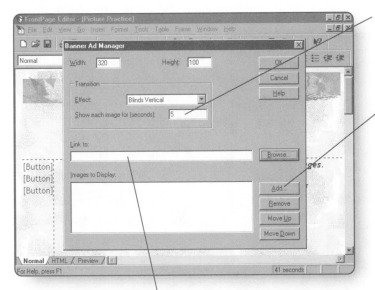

9. **Double-click** in the **Show each image for (seconds): text box** and **type** the **number** of seconds to display each image.

10. **Click** on the **Add button** to add the first image that will appear in the banner. The Add Image for Banner Ad dialog box will appear.

NOTE

You can hyperlink the banner to another Web page by typing the URL of the page in the Link to: text box. You can also click on the Browse button to locate the Web page. For help creating hyperlinks, see Chapter 11, "Working with Hyperlinks."

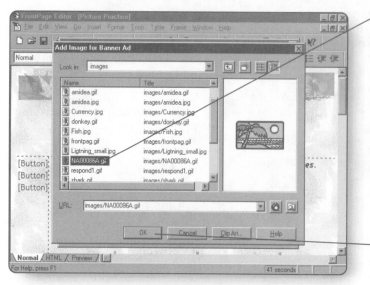

11. **Select** the **image** that you want to add to the banner. The path and file name of the image will appear in the URL: text box.

NOTE

For help finding images, see Chapter 8, "Working with Image Tools."

12. **Click** on **OK**. The image file will be added to the Images to Display: list.

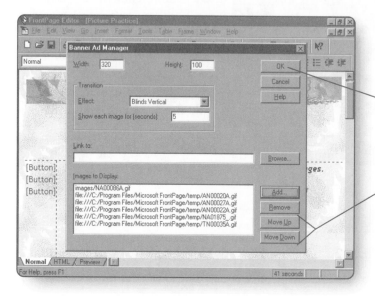

13. **Add** any additional **images**. The image files will be added to the Images to Display: list.

14. **Click** on **OK**. The banner will appear on the page.

TIP

Use the Move Up and Move Down buttons to rearrange the order of the images in the list.

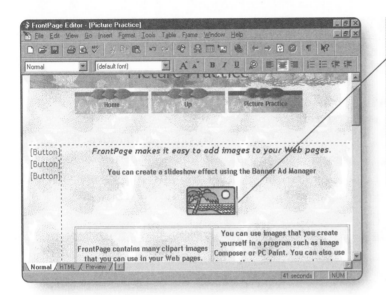

TIP

TIP

If you want to change the appearance of the banner, right-click on the banner and select Java Applet Properties. To see your banner in action, you will need to preview it in a Web browser.

ADDING A MARQUEE

Marquees are a great way to get your visitor's attention because they move text across the Web page.

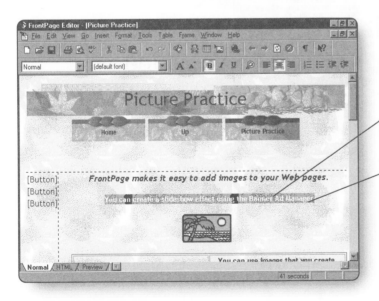

1. Open the page where you want to place the marquee. The page will display in the FrontPage Editor.

2. Type the text that you want to display in the marquee.

3. Select the text you just typed. The text will be highlighted.

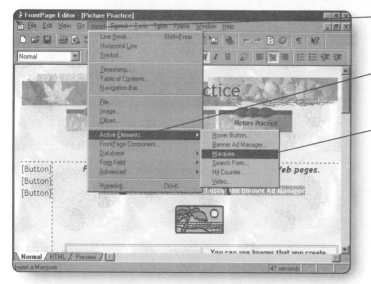

4. **Click** on **Insert**. The Insert menu will appear.

5. **Click** on **Active Elements**. Another menu will appear.

6. **Click** on **Marquee**. The Marquee Properties dialog box will appear with the selected text in the Text: text box.

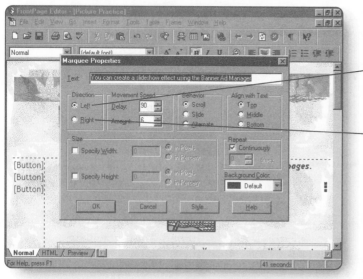

7. **Click** on a **Direction option button**:

✦ **Left** moves the marquee from the right side of the screen toward the left side.

✦ **Right** moves the marquee from the left side of the screen toward the right side.

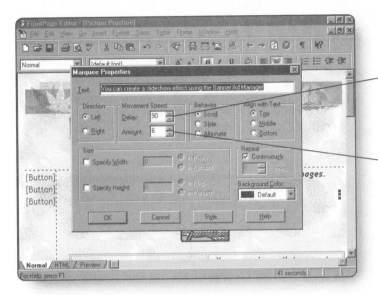

8. Click on the **Movement Speed up** and **down arrows:**

✦ **Delay:** sets the number of milliseconds before the marquee begins to move the text across the screen.

✦ **Amount:** sets the increment, measured in pixels, that the text will advance as it moves across the screen.

9. Click on a **Behavior option button:**

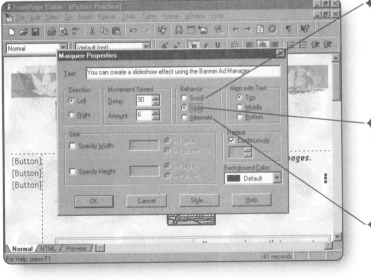

✦ **Scroll** brings the text in on one side of the screen and moves it toward the other end, where it disappears and reappears from its original entry point.

✦ **Slide** moves the text in from one side, and when the text reaches the other side of the screen, it stops and remains in this position.

✦ **Alternate** moves the text back and forth across the screen.

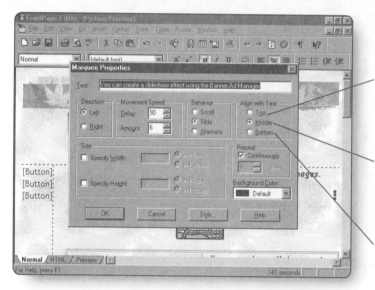

10. **Click** on an **Align with Text** option button:

✦ **Top** aligns the top of the marquee text with the top of any text that may appear on the same line.

✦ **Middle** aligns the middle of the marquee text with the middle of any text that may appear on the same line.

✦ **Bottom** aligns the bottom of the marquee text with the bottom of any text that may appear on the same line.

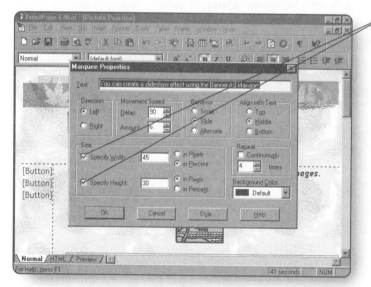

11. **Set** the **Size** of the marquee if you want the marquee border to extend beyond the marquee text:

✦ **in Pixels option button** allows you to set an exact height or width for the marquee.

✦ **in Percent option button** causes the marquee to appear in different sizes on different screens, depending on the screen size and screen resolution.

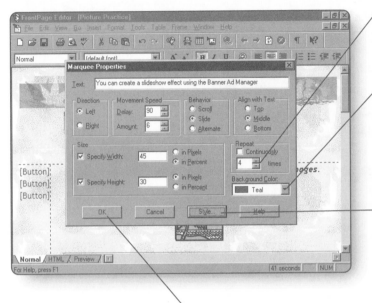

12. Select the **number** of times you want the marquee to move across the screen.

13. Click on the **down arrow** next to the Background Color: text box and **select** a **color** that will appear around the marquee text.

NOTE

If you want to experiment with your marquee, click on the Style button. Use the Borders, Font, and Colors tabs.

14. Click on OK. The marquee will appear on the page.

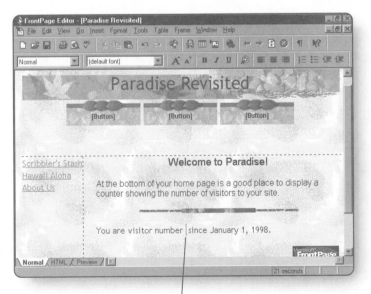

KEEPING TRACK OF YOUR VISITORS

Keeping track of the number of times a page on your Web site is accessed is easy.

1. Open the **page** you want to display the counter. The page will appear in the FrontPage Editor.

2. Click on the **place** where you want the counter to appear. The insertion bar will appear in the selected place.

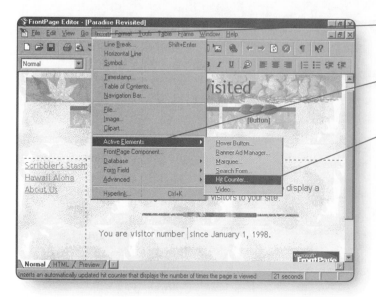

3. **Click** on **Insert**. The Insert menu will appear.

4. **Click** on **Active Elements**. A second menu will appear.

5. **Click** on **Hit Counter**. The Hit Counter Properties dialog box appears.

6. **Click** on a **Counter Style option button**. The option will be selected.

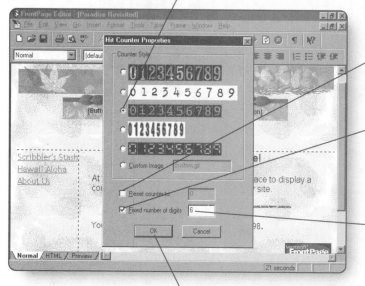

TIP

If you want to reset the counter, click on the Reset counter to check box.

7. **Click** on the **Fixed number of digits** check box to display the counter as if it were the odometer in a car.

8. **Click** in the **text box** and **type** the **number** of digits to appear in the counter.

9. **Click** on **OK**. A text holder will appear in the place you selected for the counter.

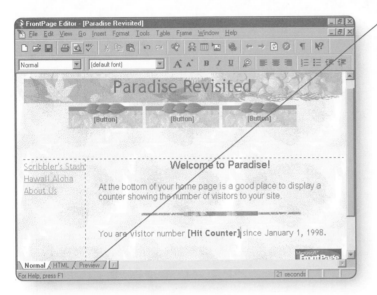

10. Click on the **Preview in Browser button**. The default Web browser opens.

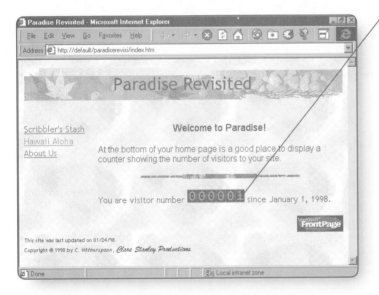

Your default Web browser will open and you can scroll to the place on the page where you positioned the counter.

10 Working with Forms

The easiest way to collect information, sell products, or conduct surveys on the Internet is by using forms. Forms on the Internet look like the paper forms you fill out all the time. Forms on the Internet were once the domain of those people who knew something about CGI programming. This is no longer the case. The folks at Microsoft have, once again, developed a way for anyone to create a form and make it functional, automatically, when the form is published to your Web site. In this chapter, you'll learn how to:

✦ Get a quick and easy start on your form

✦ Collect responses from your form page

✦ Edit your form by adding additional form fields

CREATING A FORM

The easiest way to build your form is to use the Form Page Wizard. The wizard walks you through the steps needed to create the form and suggests question topics for your visitors. The wizard generates the form and includes a way for your visitors to send their responses to you.

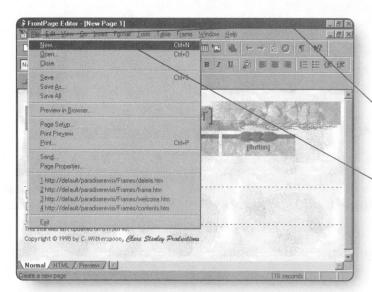

Getting Started with the Form Wizard

1. **Open** a **blank page** and **click** on **File**. The File menu will appear.

2. **Click** on **New**. The New dialog box will appear with the Page tab displayed.

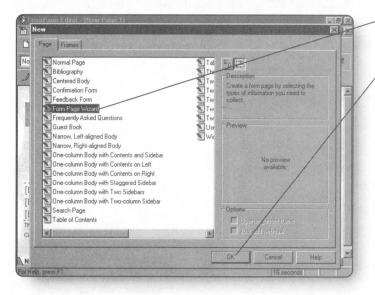

3. **Click** on **Form Page Wizard**. The wizard will be selected.

4. **Click** on **OK**. The Form Page Wizard dialog box will appear.

TIP

Besides using the Form Page Wizard, you can start your form using the Confirmation Form, Feedback Form, Guest Book, and User Registration templates.

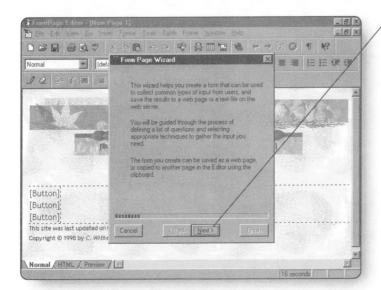

5. Click on **Next**. The next page of the wizard dialog box will appear.

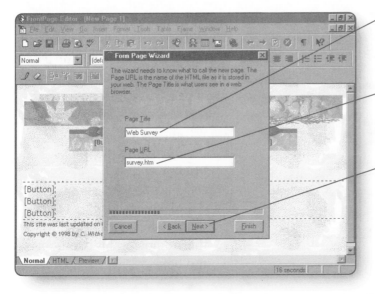

6. Double-click in the **Page Title text box** and **type** a **title** for your survey page.

7. Double-click in the **Page URL text box** and **type** a **file name** for your survey page.

8. Click on **Next**. The next page of the wizard will appear.

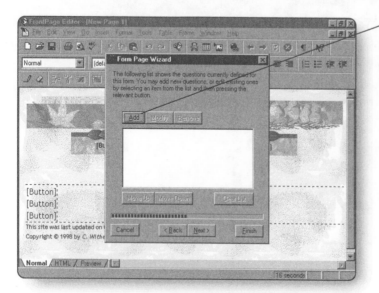

9. **Click** on the **Add button**. The next page of the wizard appears that allows you to choose from a variety of predefined form questions.

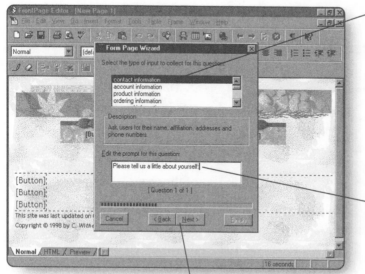

10. **Click** on a **form question** in the Select the type of input to collect for this question list. A description of the form will appear in the Description box and a sample leading question will appear in the Edit the prompt for this question: text box.

11. **Make** any **changes** to the prompt that appears in the Edit the prompt for this question: text box.

12. **Click** on **Next**. A screen asking for the type of information to collect will appear.

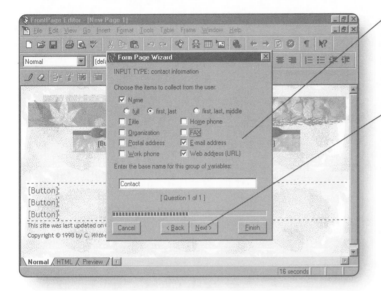

13. Put a **check mark** in the boxes associated with the information that you want to collect.

14. **Click** on **Next**. The next page of the wizard appears showing the type of input that will be collected on the form.

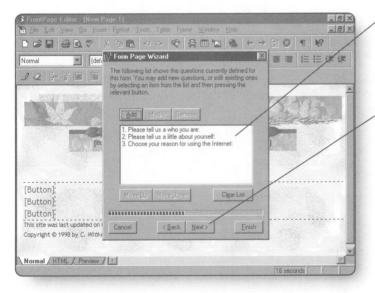

15. **Repeat steps 9-14** until all the information that you want collected on the form appears in the list.

16. **Click** on **Next**. The next page of the wizard will appear.

17. **Click** on an **option** from the How should the list of questions be presented? section. The option will be selected.

18. **Click** on an **option** from the Would you like a Table of Contents for this page? section. The option will be selected.

19. **Put** a **check mark** in the box next to use tables to align form fields if you want to determine how your form will be formatted.

20. **Click** on **Next**. The next page of the wizard will appear.

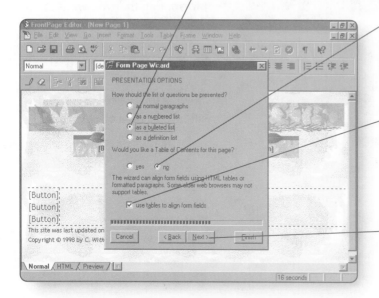

21. **Click** on an **option button** to select how you want the results of the form to be saved. The option will be selected.

22. **Double-click** in the **Enter the base name of the results file: text box** and **type** a **file name** where the results will be collected.

23. **Click** on **Next**. The last page of the wizard will appear.

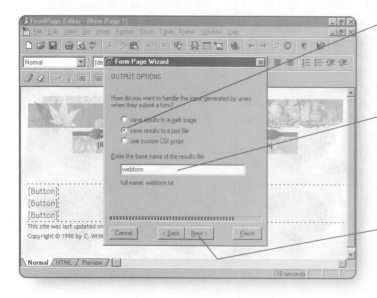

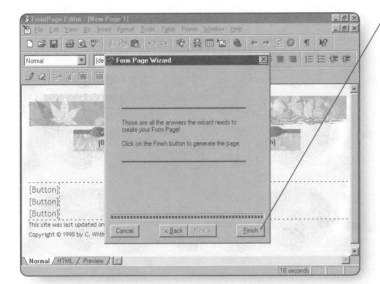

24. Click on **Finish**.

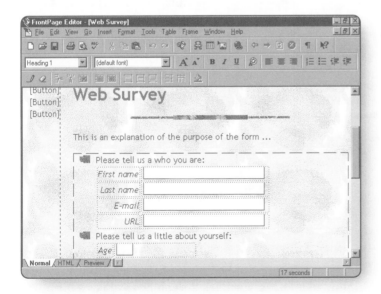

The form will appear in the FrontPage Editor.

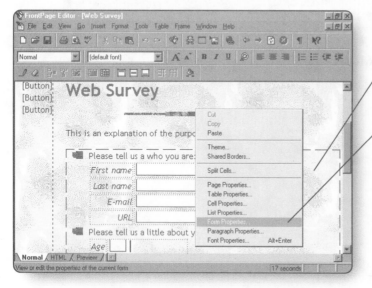

Handling Responses

1. Right-click on the **form**. A shortcut menu will appear.

2. Click on **Form Properties**. The Form Properties dialog box will appear.

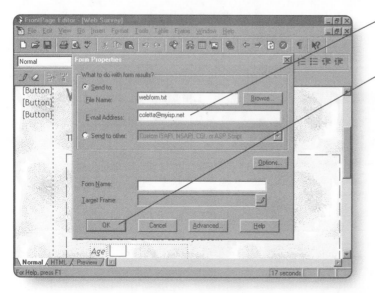

3. Type your **e-mail address** in the E-mail Address: text box.

4. Click on **OK**. When a visitor to your site submits the form, the responses will be sent to you as an e-mail message.

TIP

If your Internet Service Provider (ISP) does not support the FrontPage Server Extensions, you cannot have replies sent to your e-mail address. Form results can be saved as a file on your ISP's server along with your Web pages. You will need to use an FTP program to access your Web space and download the file to your computer. Your ISP should be able to help you with this process.

ADDING FIELDS TO THE FORM PAGE

After you have used the Form Page Wizard to create a form, you can go back and add new fields to the form. But before you do, you will want to display the Forms toolbar to make this task quicker and easier.

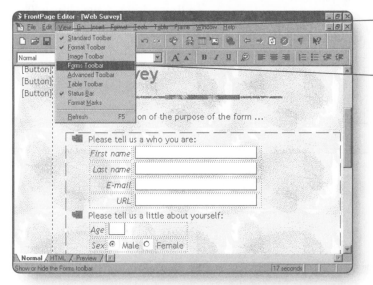

1. **Click** on **View**. The View Menu will appear.

2. **Click** on **Forms Toolbar**. The Forms Toolbar will appear.

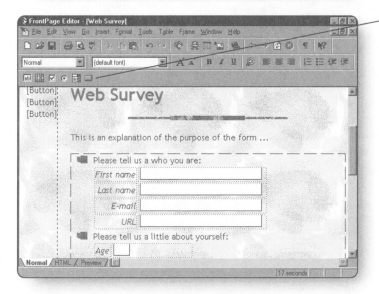

The Forms Toolbar will appear below the other toolbars that are displayed in the FrontPage Editor.

Creating a One-Line Text Box

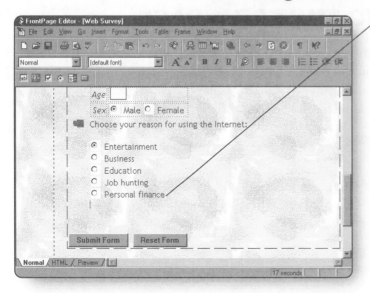

1. Click at the **end** of the line preceding the space where you want to add the new form field. The insertion bar will appear at the end of the line.

2. Press Enter. A new line will appear.

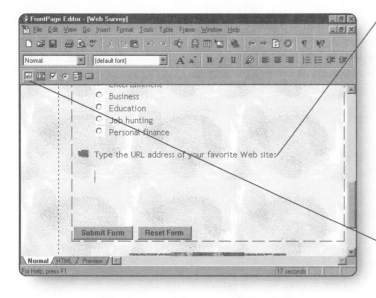

3. Type the **text** that you want to use to describe how your visitor should use the form field and **press Enter**.

> ### NOTE
> You can format and edit text in a form in the same way you format text in any Web page.

4. Click on the **One-Line Text Box button** on the Forms toolbar. A one-line form field will appear on the page.

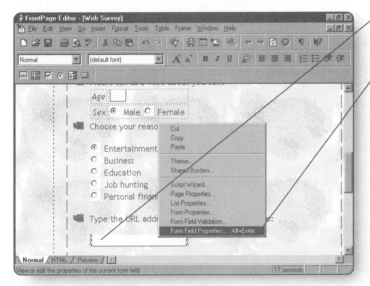

5. **Right-click** on the **text box**. A shortcut menu will appear.

6. **Click** on **Form Field Properties**. The Text Box Properties dialog box will appear.

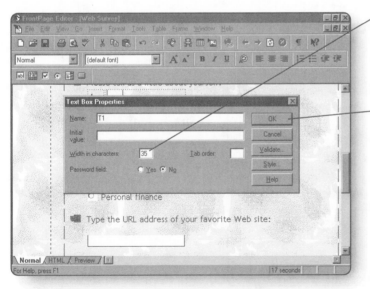

7. **Double-click** in the **Width in characters: text box** and **type** the **width**, in characters, of the desired text box.

8. **Click** on **OK**. The text box will be resized.

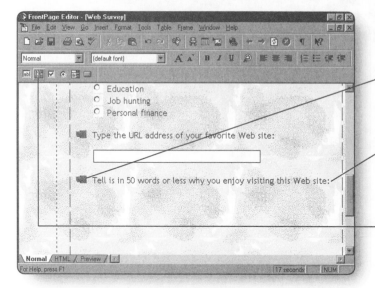

Using Scrolling Text Boxes

1. **Click** in the **place** where you want to add a scrolling text box. The insertion bar will appear.

2. **Type** the **text** that you want to use as a lead-in to the form field and **press Enter**.

3. **Click** on the **Scrolling Text Box button** on the Forms toolbar. A text box with scroll bars will appear on the page.

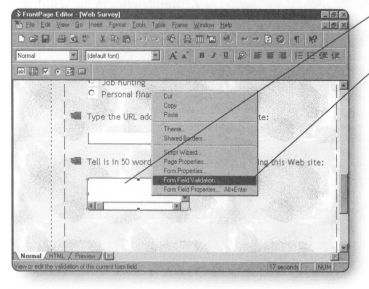

4. **Right-click** on the **scroll box**. A shortcut menu will appear.

5. **Click** on **Form Field Validation**. The Text Box Validation dialog box will appear.

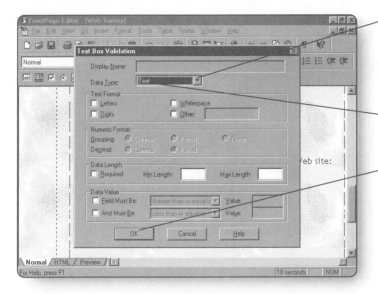

6. Click on the **down arrow** next to the Data Type: drop-down list. A list of options will appear.

7. Click on **Text**. The option will be selected.

8. Click on **OK**. Visitors to your site will only be able to type text into the scroll box.

INCLUDING BOXES AND BUTTONS

Check boxes and option buttons allow visitors to your form page to select from a variety of options. These boxes and buttons are easy to create.

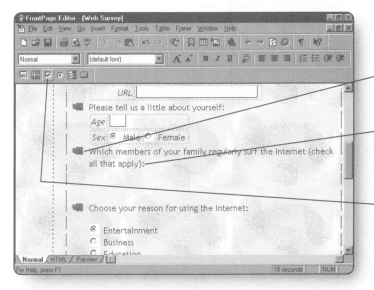

Creating Check Boxes

1. Click in the **place** where you want to add the check boxes.

2. Type the **text** that you want to use as a lead-in to the form field and **press Enter**.

3. Click on the **Check Box button** on the Forms toolbar. A check box will appear in the selected position.

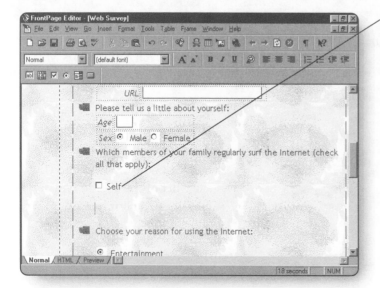

4. Type **text** to describe the purpose of the text box and **press Enter**.

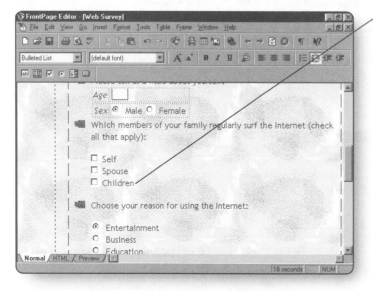

5. **Add** additional **check boxes** to complete the response options to the question.

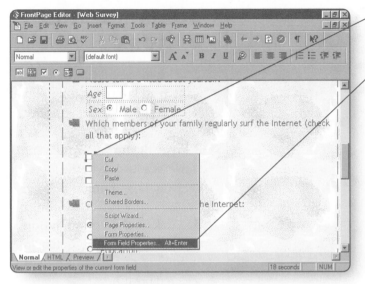

6. **Right-click** on a **check box**. A shortcut menu will appear.

7. **Click** on **Form Field Properties**. The Check Box Properties dialog box will appear.

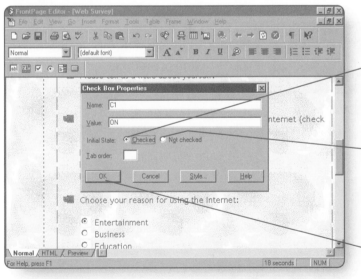

8. **Choose** one of the **options** from the Initial State: section:

✦ **Checked**. Automatically places a check mark in the check box so that your visitor does not need to do this.

✦ **Not Checked**. Leaves the check box blank, giving your visitor the option to leave the box unchecked or to check the box.

9. **Click** on **OK**. The option will be applied to the check box.

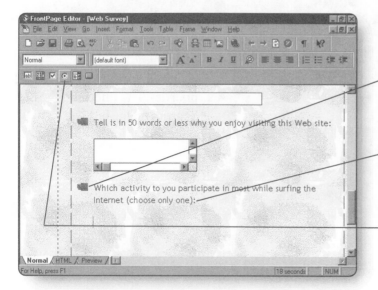

Adding Option Buttons

1. Click in the **place** where you want to add the option buttons. The insertion bar will appear.

2. Type the **text** that you want to use as a lead-in to the form field and press Enter.

3. Click on the **Option Button button** on the Forms toolbar. An option button will appear in the selected position.

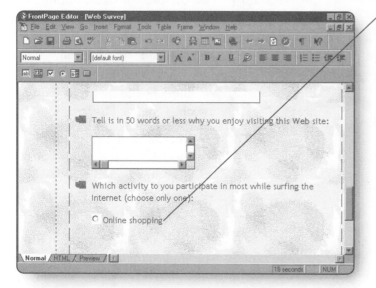

4. Type **text** to describe the purpose of the option button and press Enter.

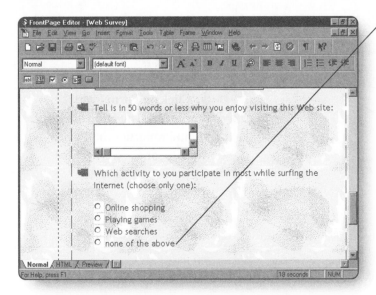

5. **Add** additional **option buttons** to complete the response options to the question.

CREATING DROP-DOWN LISTS

Drop-down lists allow you to give your visitors a number of options from which to choose. They also take up less space than check boxes or option buttons.

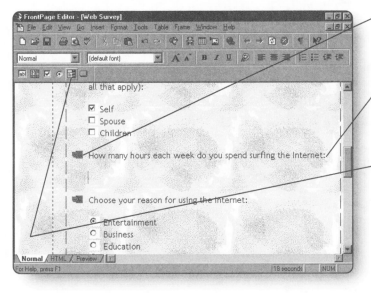

1. **Click** in the **place** where you want to add the drop-down list. The insertion bar will appear.

2. **Type** the **text** that you want to use as a lead-in to the form field and press Enter.

3. **Click** on the **Drop-Down List button** on the Forms toolbar. A drop-down list will appear in the selected position.

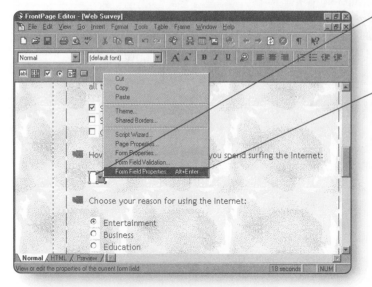

4. **Right-click** on the **drop-down list**. A shortcut menu will appear.

5. **Click** on **Form Field Properties**. The Drop-Down Menu Properties dialog box will appear.

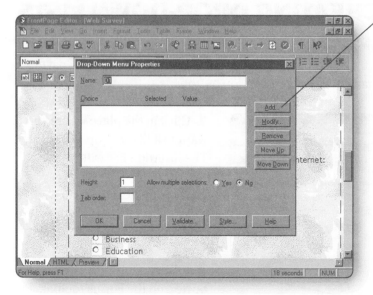

6. **Click** on the **Add button**. The Add Choice dialog box will appear.

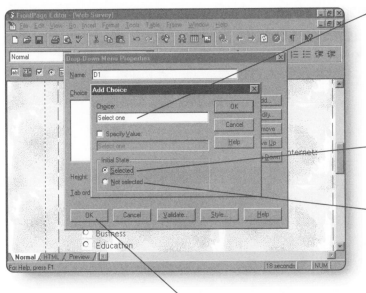

7. **Type** the **text** in the Choice: text box that you want to appear in the drop-down list.

8. **Choose** one of the **options** in the Initial State section:

✦ **Selected**. This text will appear in the text box that displays in the drop-down list.

✦ **Not Selected**. This text will be hidden until the visitor clicks on the down arrow next to the drop-down list.

9. **Click** on **OK**. The text will be added to the Drop-Down Menu Properties dialog box.

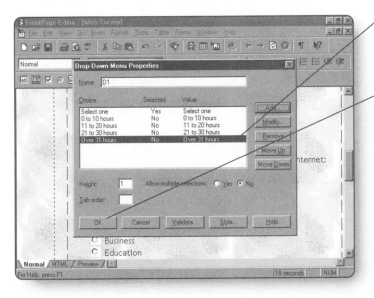

10. **Add** additional **choices** that you want to appear in the drop-down list.

11. **Click** on **OK**. The drop-down list will be created.

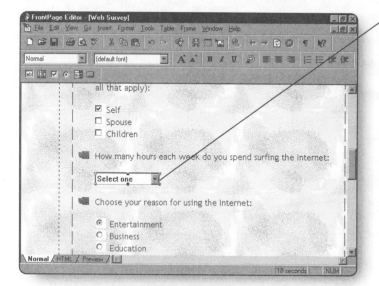

The drop-down list.

PART III REVIEW QUESTIONS

1. Where can you find pictures that you can use on your Web pages? *See "Inserting Images" in Chapter 8.*

2. What are three different effects that you can apply to your images to make them look different? *See "Editing Images" in Chapter 8.*

3. How do you add your own images to the Clip Gallery? *See "Adding Images to the Clip Gallery" in Chapter 8.*

4. Does FrontPage give you the ability to use your own images to create hover buttons? *See "Using Hover Buttons" in Chapter 9.*

5. How can you create a slideshow on a Web page? *See "Creating Banners" in Chapter 9.*

6. What are the two ways that you can make text move around on a Web page? *See "Adding a Marquee" in Chapter 9.*

7. What are the four form templates included with FrontPage? *See "Getting Started with the Form Wizard" in Chapter 10.*

8. How do you display the Forms toolbar to make building forms easier? *See "Adding Fields to the Form Page" in Chapter 10.*

9. What are the two types of text boxes that you can add to a form? *See "Adding Fields to the Form Page" in Chapter 10.*

10. If you want to conserve space on your Web page, what is the best type of form field to use? *See "Creating Drop-Down Lists" in Chapter 10.*

PART IV
Linking your Web

gif
a.jpg
ey.gif
a.jpg
ntpag.gi
ish.jpg
respond.gi
shark.gif
sunset.gif

URL: imag

HTML / Preview /

11 Working with Hyperlinks

Hyperlinks glue your web together and keep it connected to the Internet. Hyperlinks can take your visitors to any page at your site that you want them to see. Hyperlinks let you share some of your favorite places on the Internet or direct visitors to places where they can find more information about a subject discussed in your web. If you want to give visitors an easy way to correspond with you, you can create a hyperlink that will address an e-mail message to you. In this chapter, you'll learn how to:

✦ Direct visitors to pages in your Web site and other interesting sites.

✦ Help your visitors navigate your web.

✦ Make changes to hyperlinks that you've already created.

CREATING LINKS TO PAGES ON THE WEB

If you have some favorite Web sites that you want to share with your visitors, you can make it easy for them by creating a hyperlink. With the click of a mouse button, your visitor will enjoy the same Web sites you found so fascinating. Before you create a hyperlink to a Web site, you should check with the owner of the site and ask his permission to link. You can find out if he is willing to allow this by looking through the Web site or by sending a short e-mail message. Most Web site owners will gladly comply with the request, but some may have restrictions.

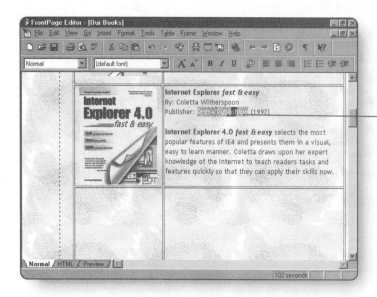

1. **Open** the **page** that will contain the link to the Web site. The page will appear in the FrontPage Editor Window.

2. Select the **text** or **graphic** that you want to use as the link. The text or graphic will be highlighted.

TIP

The easiest way to create a hyperlink is to type the URL address on the page you are linking from in the FrontPage Editor. FrontPage automatically turns the text into a link.

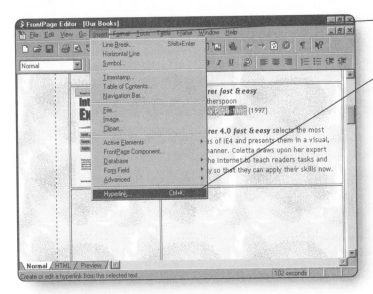

3. Click on **Insert**. The Insert menu will appear.

4. Click on **Hyperlink**. The Create Hyperlink dialog box will appear.

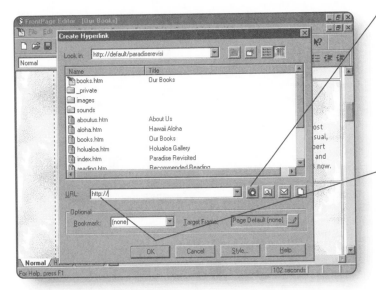

5. Click on the **Use Your Web Browser to Select a Page or File button**. Your default Web browser will open.

TIP

If you know the URL address of the Web page to which you want to create a hyperlink, type it in the URL: text box.

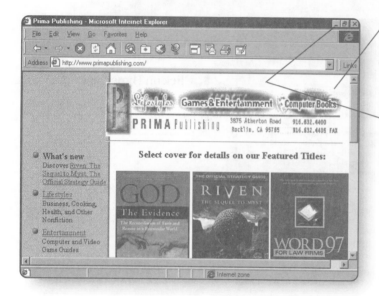

6. **Navigate** to the **Web page** to which you want to create a link. The Web page will appear in the Web browser window.

7. **Click** on the **Minimize button**. The Edit Hyperlink dialog box will appear with the URL of the Web page in the URL: text box.

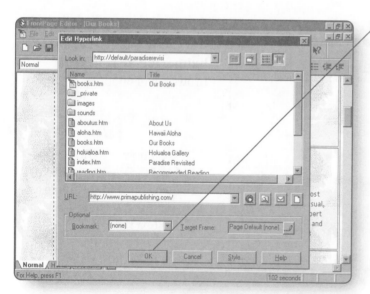

8. **Click** on **OK**. The hyperlink will be created.

TIP

On pages that contain numerous links to sites on the World Wide Web, you may want to add a note to the page that reminds your visitors to use the Back button on their browser to return to your site.

CREATING LINKS INSIDE YOUR WEB

Navigation bars (which you learned about in Chapter 5) provide one way to move around a Web site. You can also use hyperlinks to browse from page to page within a web. These hyperlinks can point a visitor to specific pages or places on a page, and open a word processing or slide show file in a visitor's browser. If you can put it in your web, you can create a link that points to it.

Creating a Link to a New Page

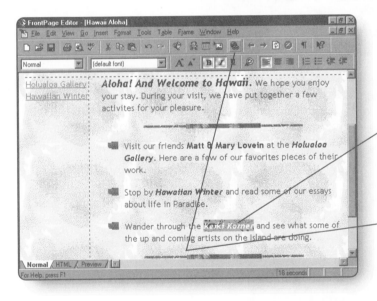

1. Open the **page** that will contain the link to the page within your web. The page will appear in the FrontPage Editor Window.

2. Select the **text** or **graphic** that you want to use as the link. The text or graphic will be highlighted.

3. Click on the **Create or Edit Hyperlink button**. The Create Hyperlink dialog box will appear.

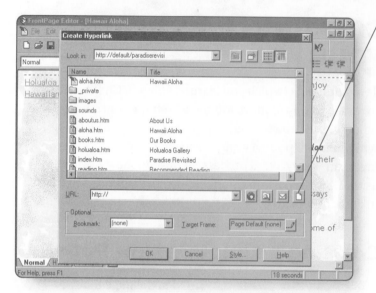

4. **Click** on the **Create a Page and Link to the New Page button.** The New dialog box will appear.

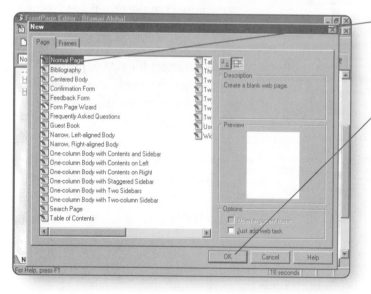

5. **Click** on the **template page** that you want to use for the new page. The template will appear in the Preview pane.

6. **Click** on **OK.** The new page will appear in the FrontPage Editor window.

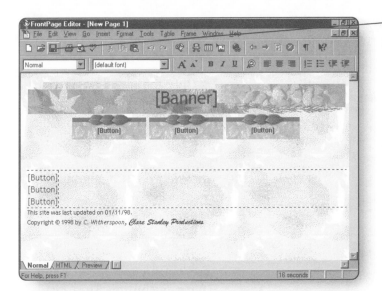

7. Click on the **Save button**. The Save As dialog box will appear.

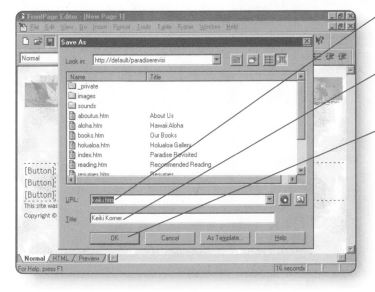

8. Type a **file name** for the new page in the URL: text box.

9. Type a **title** for the page in the Title: text box.

10. Click on **OK**. The page is now linked to your web.

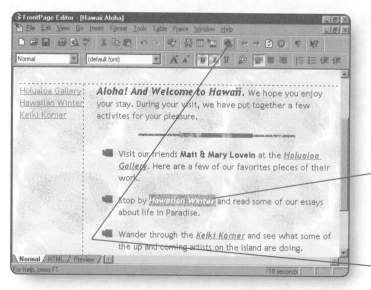

Linking to an Existing Page

1. **Open** the **page** that will contain the link to the page within your web. The page will appear in the FrontPage Editor Window.

2. **Select** the **text** or **graphic** that you want to use as the link. The text or graphic will be highlighted.

3. **Click** on the **Create or Edit Hyperlink button**. The Create Hyperlink dialog box will appear.

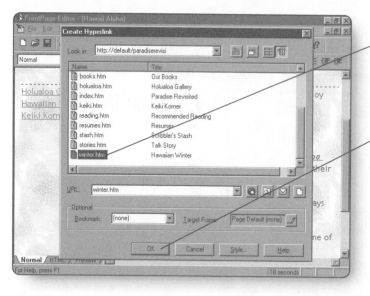

4. **Click** on the **page** to which you want to create the link. The file name will appear in the URL: text box.

5. **Click** on **OK**. The hyperlink will be created.

NOTE

If you create an image hyperlink, by default a box will appear around the image. This allows you to recognize image hyperlinks while you are working in the FrontPage Editor. Also, this box informs visitors to your site that an image contains a hyperlink. You can change this default setting by right-clicking on the image, choosing Image Properties, clicking on the Appearance tab, and setting the Border Thickness: to 0.

Creating Links to Bookmarks

Bookmarks allow you to create hyperlinks that will take your visitor to a specific place on a specific page within your web. Bookmarks work well if you have a large amount of information on a page and you don't want to make your visitor wade through all of it. Creating these types of hyperlinks involves a two step process. First, you create the bookmark, and then you create the hyperlink that will direct the visitor to the bookmark.

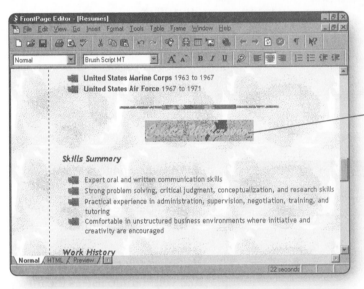

1. Open the **page** that will contain the bookmark. The page will appear in the FrontPage Editor Window.

2. Select the **text or graphic** that you want to use as the bookmark. The text or graphic will be highlighted.

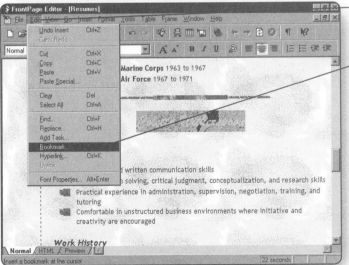

3. Click on **Edit**. The Edit menu will appear.

4. Click on **Bookmark**. The Bookmark dialog box will appear.

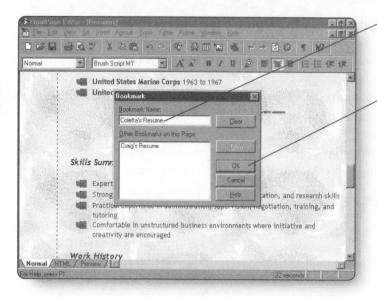

5. Type a **name** for the bookmark in the Bookmark Name: text box.

6. **Click** on **OK**. The bookmark will be created. Now that you have created the bookmark, it is time to create the hyperlink that will direct your visitors to the bookmark.

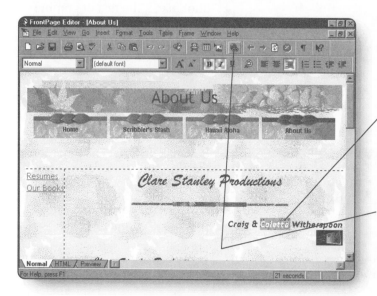

7. **Open** the **page** that will contain the link to the bookmark. The page will appear in the FrontPage Editor.

8. **Select** the **text** or **graphic** that you want to use as the link. The text or graphic will be highlighted.

9. **Click** on the **Create or Edit Hyperlink button**. The Create Hyperlink dialog box will appear.

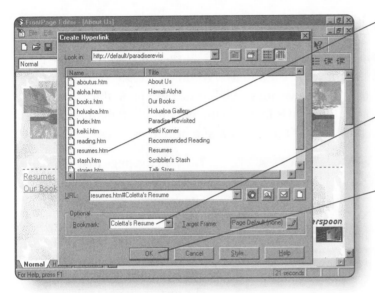

10. Click on the **page** that contains the bookmark to which you want to create a link. The page will be selected.

11. Type the **name of the bookmark** in the Bookmark: text box.

12. Click on **OK**. The link to the bookmark will be created.

NOTE

If the hyperlink is contained on the same page as the bookmark, click on the down arrow next to the Bookmark: text box and select the bookmark to which the hyperlink will point.

Linking to files

You may have a Microsoft Word, Excel, or PowerPoint file that you want your visitor to use. When you create a link to one of these files, the visitor's Web browser will open the associated application (if it is installed on his computer) or open a viewer so that your visitor can view and print these files.

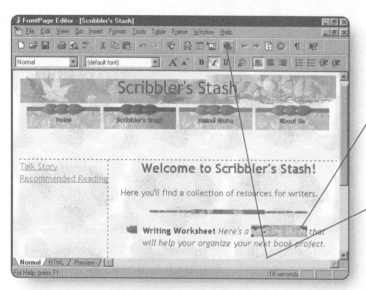

1. Open the **page** that will contain the link to the file. The page will appear in the FrontPage Editor.

2. Select the **text** or **graphic** that you want to use as the link. The text or graphic will be highlighted.

3. Click on the **Create or Edit Hyperlink button**. The Create Hyperlink dialog box will appear.

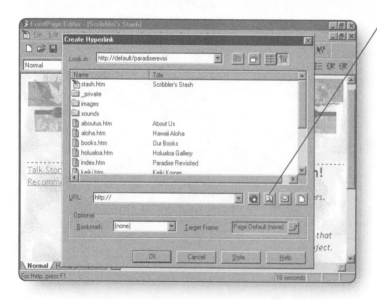

4. Click on the **Make a hyperlink to a file on your computer button**. The Select File dialog box will appear.

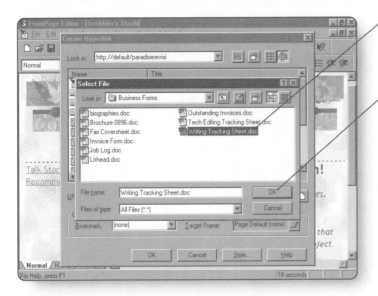

5. Click on the **file** to which you want to create the link. The file will be selected.

6. Click on **OK**. The hyperlink to the file will be created.

CREATING E-MAIL LINKS

E-mail hyperlinks make it easy for visitors to your Web site to contact you. When a visitor clicks on the e-mail link, his default e-mail program will start, open a new message window, and enter your e-mail address in the "To" field. All your visitor needs to do is type a message and press the Send button.

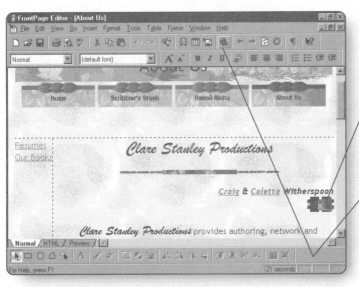

1. Select the **text** or **graphic** to which you want to create the e-mail hyperlink. The text or graphic will be highlighted.

2. Click on the **Create or Edit Hyperlink button**. The Create Hyperlink dialog box will appear.

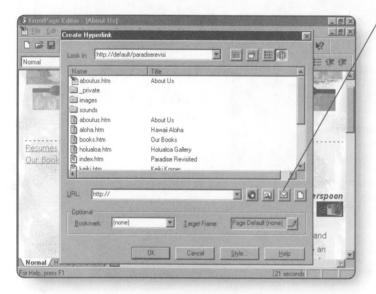

3. **Click** on the **Make a Hyperlink that Sends E-mail button**. The Create E-mail Hyperlink dialog box will appear.

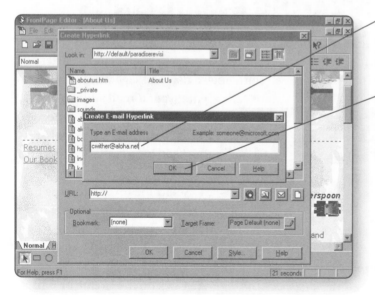

4. **Type** the **e-mail address** to which you want visitors to your site to send e-mail.

5. **Click** on **OK**. The Create Hyperlink dialog box will appear showing the hyperlink address in the URL: text box.

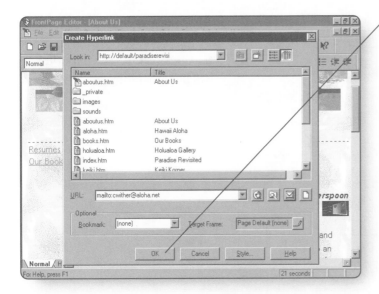

6. **Click** on **OK**. The e-mail hyperlink will be created.

MAKING CHANGES TO HYPERLINKS

Once a hyperlink has been created, it's easy to change the address of the page to which the link points.

1. **Click** on the **hyperlink** that you want to edit. The hyperlink will be selected.

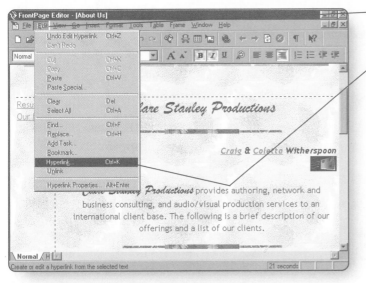

2. **Click** on **Edit**. The Edit menu will appear.

3. **Click** on **Hyperlink**. The Edit Hyperlink dialog box will appear.

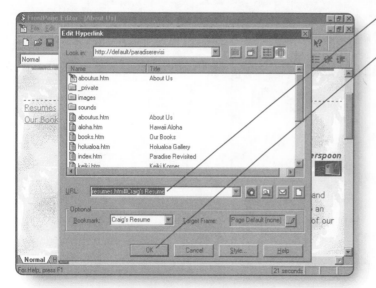

4. **Make** any **changes** you need.

5. **Click** on **OK**. The hyperlink will be updated.

SELECTING HYPERLINK COLORS

You can change the color scheme that is used to display hyperlinks. Visitors use these colors to determine whether they have followed the various links to visit certain pages.

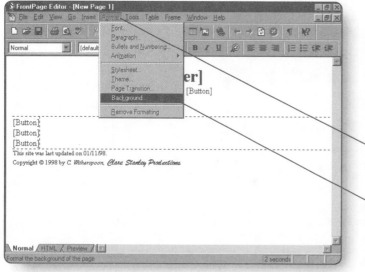

NOTE

You cannot change the hyperlink colors if you are using one of the FrontPage themes.

1. **Click** on **Format**. The Format menu will appear.

2. **Click** on **Background**. The Page Properties dialog box will appear with the Background tab displayed.

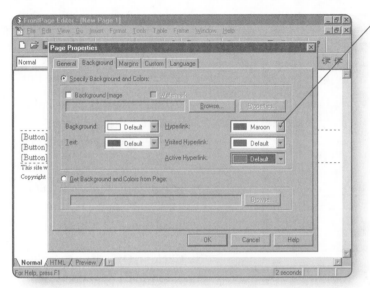

3. Click on the **down arrow** next to the hyperlink colors list box. A list of colors will appear.

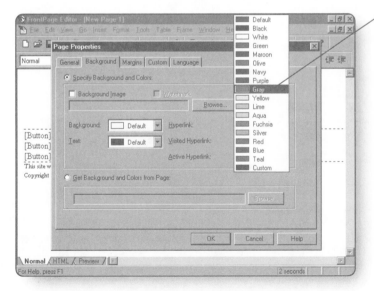

4. Click on a **color**. The color will appear in the list box.

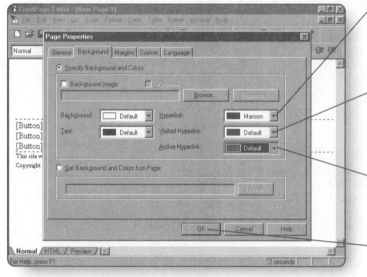

✦ **Hyperlink**. The color displayed when visitors to the Web site have not accessed the page specified by the link.

✦ **Visited Hyperlink**. The color displayed after a visitor accesses the page specified by the link.

✦ **Active Hyperlink**. The color displayed when a visitor clicks on a hyperlink.

5. **Click** on **OK**. The new color scheme will be applied.

12 Working with Graphics

As you learned in the previous chapter, you can use your images to create graphical hyperlinks. When you use an image as the link to other Web pages, you'll want the image to resemble the main theme of the page to which it is linked. This is one way of making it easier for your visitors to navigate your Web site. You'll also want to create pages that appear in your visitor's Web browser quickly. In this chapter, you'll learn how to:

✦ Adjust how images will appear when viewed on the World Wide Web

✦ Create thumbnail views of images for faster display

✦ Build image maps

DISPLAYING IMAGES ON THE WEB

Graphical images work very well as hyperlinks. Creating a hyperlink using a graphical image is as easy as creating a hyperlink using text. But there are a few extra tricks you can learn to make your graphical hyperlinks more descriptive and appealing to your visitors.

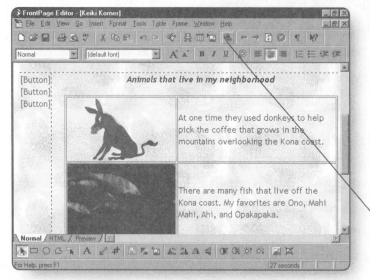

Creating an Image Hyperlink

1. **Click** on the **image** that you want to serve as the hyperlink. The image will be selected.

2. **Click** on the **Create or Edit Hyperlink button**. The Create Hyperlink dialog box will appear.

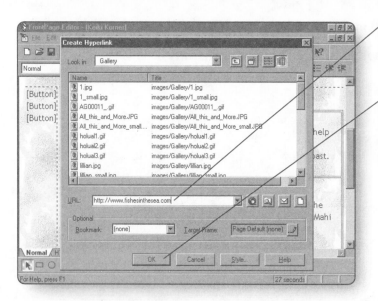

3. **Type** the **URL** of the Web page to which you want to create the hyperlink.

4. **Click** on **OK**. A colored border will appear around the image indicating that a hyperlink has been created.

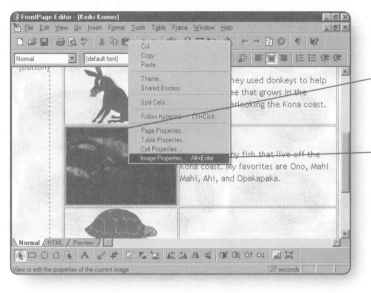

Adjusting the Image Border

1. **Right-click** on the **image** that is surrounded by a border. A shortcut menu will appear.

2. **Click** on **Image Properties**. The Image Properties dialog box will appear with the General tab displayed.

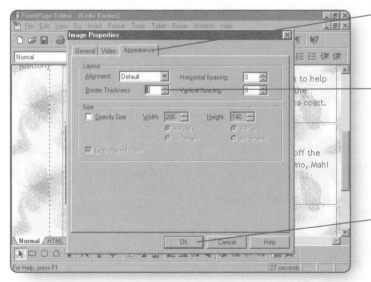

3. **Click** on the **Appearance tab**. The Appearance tab will come forward.

4. **Click** on the **up** and **down arrows** to select the border thickness that you want to appear around the image. The number in the text box will change.

5. **Click** on **OK**. The border around the image will become thinner or thicker depending on the border thickness you chose.

Using Low Resolution Images

If you have added an image to your Web page that has a large file size (and correspondingly, a long download time), you may want to add an alternative image. By adding an alternative (lower resolution and file size) image, visitors to your site will have something to look at while they are waiting for the larger image to download. After the larger image has downloaded, it will replace the lower resolution image.

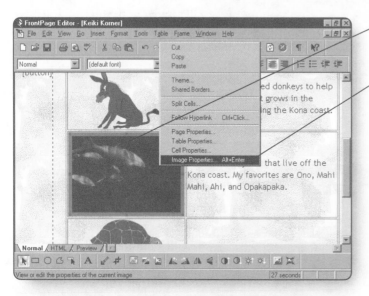

1. **Right-click** on the **image**. A shortcut menu will appear.

2. **Click** on **Image Properties**. The Image Properties dialog box will appear with the General tab displayed.

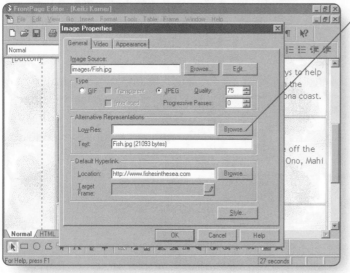

3. **Click** on the **Browse button** in the Alternative Representations section. The Select Alternate Image dialog box will appear.

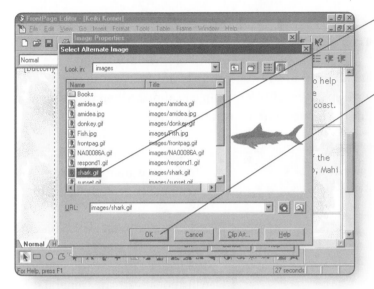

4. Select a **low-resolution image**. The image will be selected.

5. Click on **OK**. The path and file name for the image will appear in the Low-Res: text box of the Image Properties dialog box.

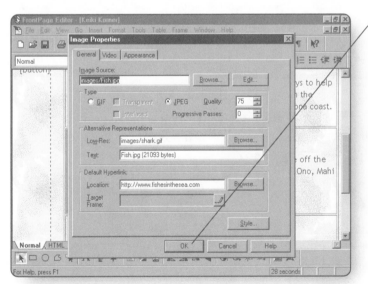

6. Click on **OK**. When a visitor accesses the page, the lower resolution image will appear first in the visitor's Web browser and will display until the higher-resolution image completely downloads.

Attaching Screen Messages to Images

You may want to add a screentip to any images you place on your Web pages. This screentip will appear when your visitor holds the mouse pointer over the image.

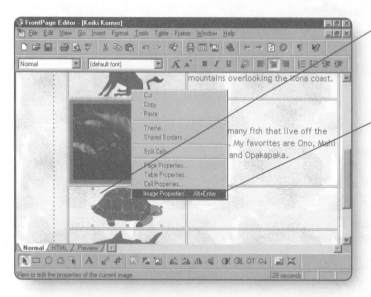

1. **Right-click** on the **image** to which you want to attach a screen message. A shortcut menu will appear.

2. **Click** on **Image Properties**. The Image Properties dialog box will appear with the General tab displayed.

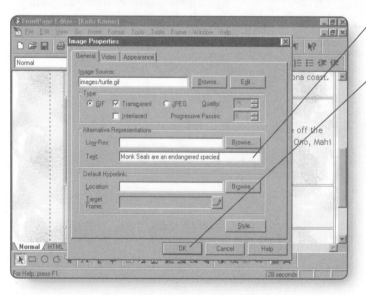

3. **Type** a **message** in the Text: text box.

4. **Click** on **OK**. The screen message will be added to the image.

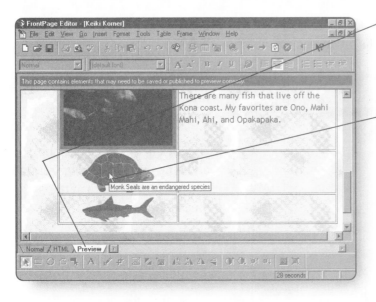

5. **Click** on the **Preview tab** at the bottom left of the FrontPage Editor window. The Preview window will appear.

6. **Hold** the **mouse pointer** over the image. The screen message will appear.

CREATING THUMBNAIL VIEWS

There may be times when you insert an image into a Web page, only to find that the image takes up most of the page. You could resize the image, but your visitors would not be able to see the detail in the image. One solution is to create thumbnails.

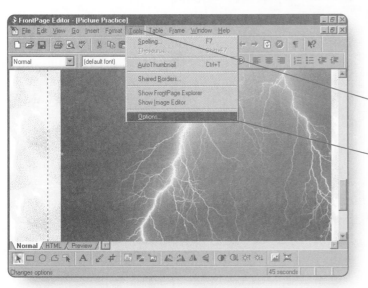

Thumbnails take up a small space on a Web page while giving your visitors the opportunity to see the larger picture at their option.

1. **Click** on **Tools**. The Tools menu will appear.

2. **Click** on **Options**. The Options dialog box will appear with the Auto Thumbnail tab displayed.

3. **Click** on the **down arrow** to the right of the Set: text box. A list of measurement units will appear.

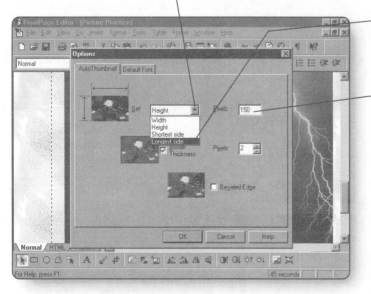

4. **Click** on a **measurement unit**. The measurement unit will be selected.

5. **Click** in the **Pixels: text box** and **type** the **number** of pixels to be used for the width of the measurement unit.

NOTE

When you set the number of pixels for one side of a thumbnail image, FrontPage will automatically set the length of the other side so that the thumbnail maintains the same aspect ratio as the original image.

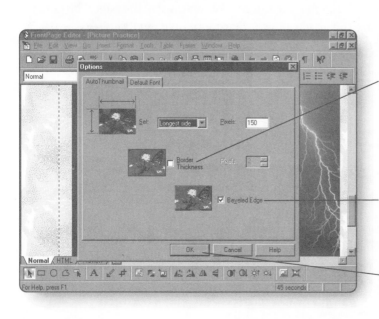

6. **Choose** from the following **options**:

✦ **Border Thickness**. To add a border around the image, click on Border Thickness and then click on the up and down arrows to set the border thickness.

✦ **Beveled Edge**. To add a bevel edge to the thumbnail image, click on Beveled Edge.

7. **Click** on **OK**. All of the thumbnails that you create will take on the appearance specified.

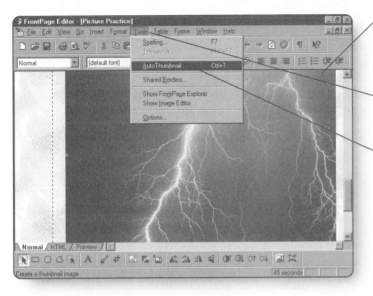

8. Click on the **image** that you want to be a thumbnail. The image will be selected.

9. Click on **Tools**. The Tools menu will appear.

10. Click on **Auto Thumbnail**. The thumbnail will be created.

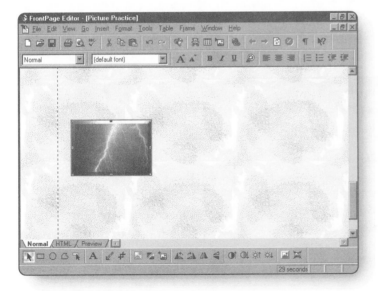

NOTE

When a visitor accesses the page, he will see the thumbnail. When he clicks on the thumbnail, another page will appear in the browser that is the full size image.

DESIGNING IMAGE MAPS

An image map starts as a piece of artwork that you create from scanned photographs, computer drawings, or clip art. The artwork is created in a computer graphics program, such as Microsoft Image Composer. You will need to create this piece of artwork using the GIF or JPEG format. This image is then inserted into a Web page, where you add hotspots to the image to create the image map. These *hotspots* are hyperlinks to other pages within your web.

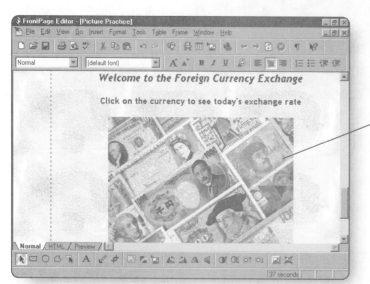

1. **Insert** the **image** that you want to use on the page.

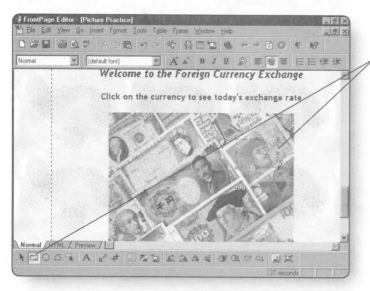

2. **Choose** a **hotspot**:

✦ To create a hotspot over a rectangular shape, click on the Rectangle button, click in the image at the upper-left of the area that you want to draw the rectangle around, and drag to the lower-right.

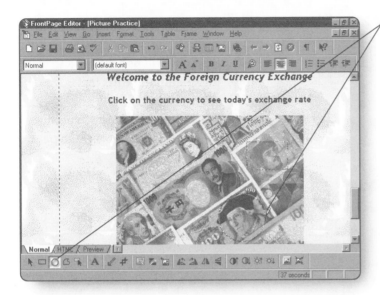

✦ To create a hotspot over a round shape, click on the Circle button, click in the image at the center of the area you want to draw the circle around, and drag away from the center point.

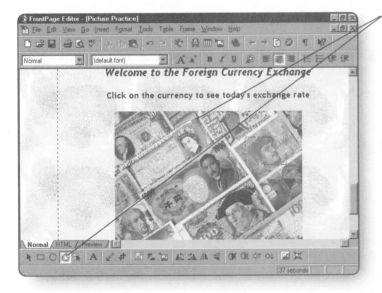

✦ To create a hotspot over an irregular shape, click on the Polygon button, click on the image at the first corner of the area, and click at each additional corner.

3. **Double-click** on the **shape**. The Create Hyperlink dialog box will appear.

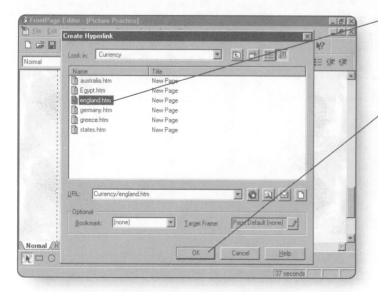

4. **Click** on the **page** to which you want to create the hyperlink. The file will be selected and will appear in the URL: text box.

5. **Click** on **OK**. The hyperlink to the corresponding Web page will be created.

6. **Click** on the **Preview tab**. The Preview window will appear.

7. **Place** the **mouse pointer** over a hotspot area. The hyperlink will appear in the Status bar at the lower-left corner of the Preview window.

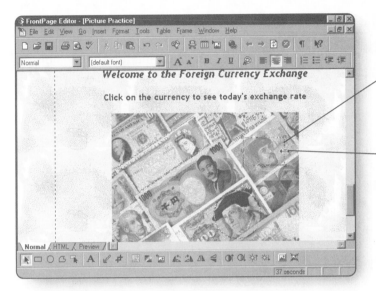

Changing the Size of a Hotspot

1. **Click** on the **hotspot** that you want to resize. The hotspot will be selected.

2. **Place** the **mouse pointer** over one of the image handles. The mouse pointer will turn into a double arrow.

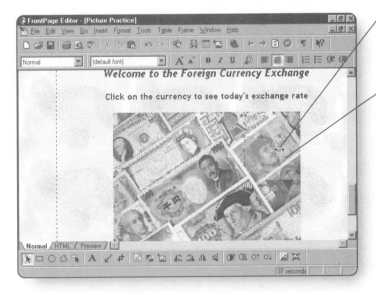

3. **Click** and **hold** the **mouse button** and **drag** the hotspot outline to the desired position.

4. **Release** the **mouse button**. The hotspot will be resized.

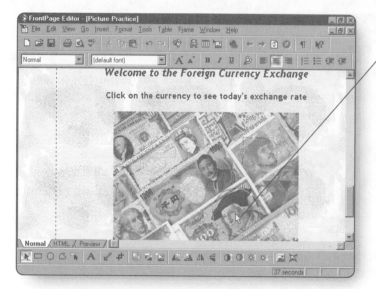

Moving Hotspots

1. **Click** and **hold** on the hotspot that you want to move. The hotspot will be selected.

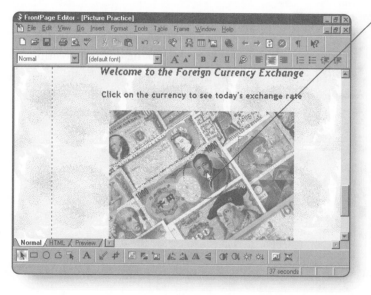

2. **Drag** the **hotspot** to the new position and **release** the **mouse button**. The hotspot will be moved.

TIP

If you begin to move a hotspot and then decide you don't want it moved, press the Escape key while clicking and dragging the hotspot.

Displaying Hotspot Outlines

If you want your visitors to be able to see where the hotspots are in your image map, you can highlight them.

1. Click on the **image map**. The image map will be selected.

2. Click on the **Highlight Hotspots button**.

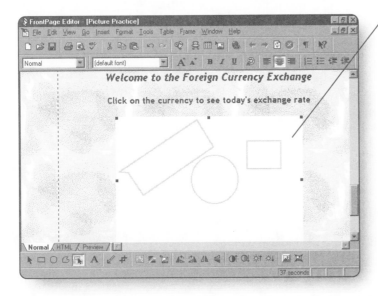

The image will appear as a blank space, with the hotspots outlined inside the space.

13 Working with Frames

You've already learned a couple of methods that make it easy for your visitors to move from page to page—hyperlinks and navigation buttons. You can also do this with frames. Frames separate the Web browser window into several separate areas. Each of these areas contains separate pages. The most common use of frames is a double layout where one frame provides the navigation element of the page and the other page contains Web page content. When a visitor to your site clicks on a link in the navigation frame, the corresponding page appears in the other frame. In this chapter, you'll learn how to:

✦ Build a basic frames page

✦ Modify the look and feel of the frames page

✦ Add and delete frames from the frames page

CREATING THE FRAMES PAGE

A frames page consists of the navigation frame and the Web pages that will be linked to the content frame. Before you begin creating your frames page, you should create the Web pages that will be linked to it. You can create the pages while you are building the frames page, but it is much easier to have these pages done in advance. This section will show you how to create a simple frames page.

Getting Your Web Pages Ready for the Frames Page

1. **Open** the **page** that you want to use in the frames page. The page will appear in the FrontPage Editor.

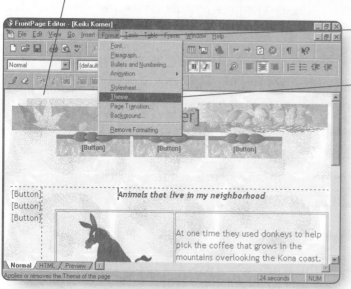

2. **Click** on **Format**. The Format menu will appear.

3. **Click** on **Theme**. The Choose Theme dialog box will appear.

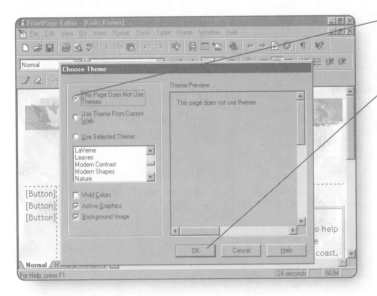

4. **Click** on the **This Page Does Not Use Themes option button**. The option will be selected.

5. **Click** on **OK**. The theme elements will be removed from the Web page.

6. **Click** on **Tools**. The Tools menu will appear.

7. **Click** on **Shared Borders**. The Page Borders dialog box will appear.

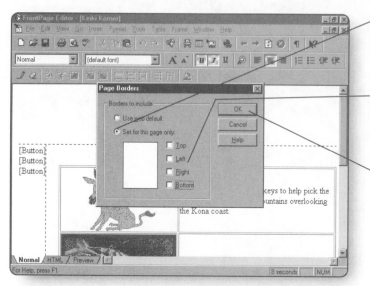

8. **Click** on the **Set for this page only: option button**. The option will be selected.

9. **Clear** the **Top**, **Left**, **Right**, and **Bottom check boxes**. The boxes will be blank.

10. **Click** on **OK**. The shared borders will be removed from the Web page.

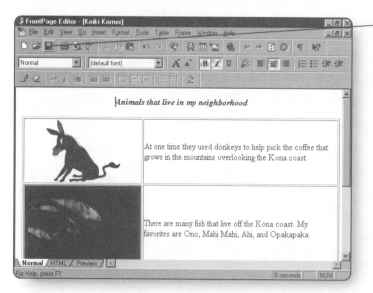

11. **Click** on the **Save** button. The Web page will be saved and is ready to be included in the frames page.

Building the Basic Frames Page

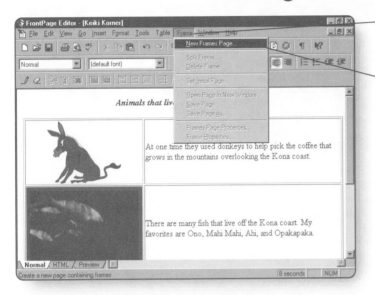

1. **Click** on **Frame**. The Frame menu will appear.

2. **Click** on **New Frames Page**. The New dialog box will appear with the Frames tab forward.

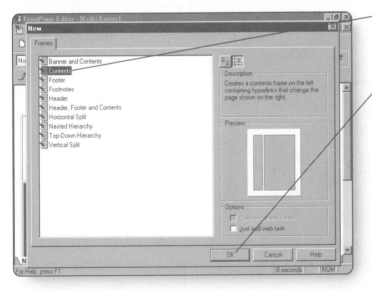

3. **Click** on the **style** of frame that you want to build. The template will be selected.

4. **Click** on **OK**. The frame template will appear in the FrontPage Editor.

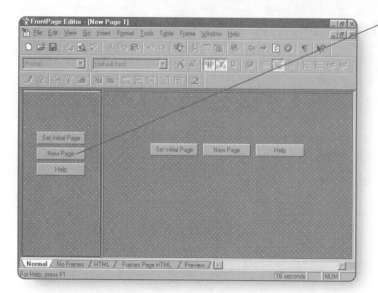

5. **Click** on the **New Page button** in the navigation frame. A blank page will appear in the frame area.

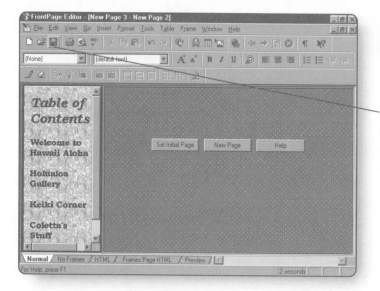

6. **Create** the **content** that you want to appear in the frame when the page appears in your visitor's browser.

7. **Click** on the **Save button**. The Save As dialog box will appear with the frame highlighted in the preview pane.

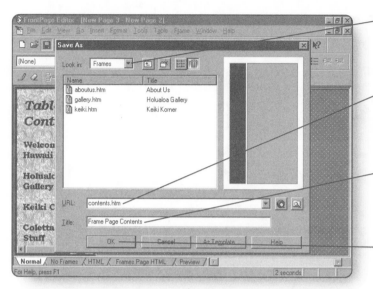

8. Click on the **folder** where you want to save the frames page. The folder will be selected.

9. Type a **file name** for this portion of the frames page in the URL: text box.

10. Type a **title** for this portion of the frames page in the Title: text box.

11. Click on **OK**. The Save As dialog box will reappear.

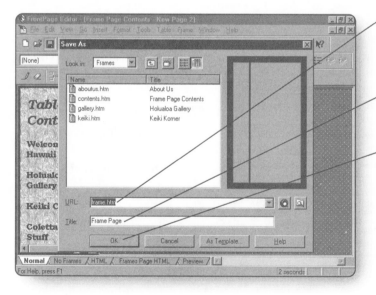

12. Type a **file name** for the frames page in the URL: text box.

13. Type a **title** for the frames page in the Title: text box.

14. Click on **OK**. The frames page will be saved.

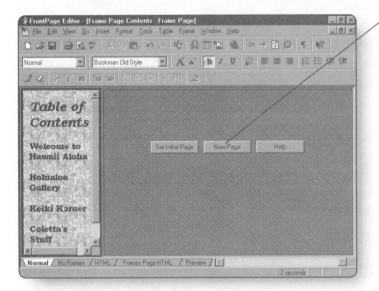

15. **Click** on the **New Page button** in all the remaining content frames. A blank page will appear in the frame area.

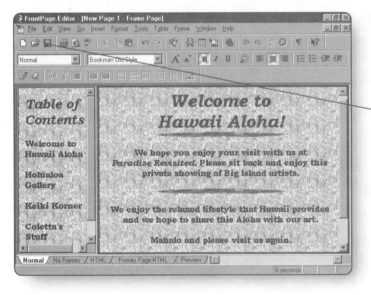

16. **Create** the **content** that you want to appear in the frame when the page appears in your visitor's browser.

17. **Click** on the **Save** button. The Save As dialog box will appear with the frame highlighted in the preview pane.

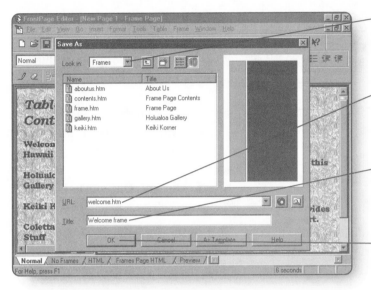

18. Click on the **folder** where you want to save the frames page. The folder will be selected.

19. Type a **file name** for this portion of the frames page in the URL: text box.

20. Type a **title** for this portion of the frames page in the Title: text box.

21. Click on **OK**. The frame will be saved and the basic structure of your frames page is finished.

Linking Web Pages to the Frames Page

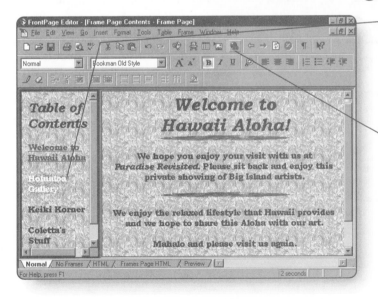

1. Select an **item** in the navigation frame that will link to a Web page that will appear in the content frame. The item will be highlighted.

2. Click on the **Create or Edit Hyperlink button**. The Create Hyperlink dialog box will appear.

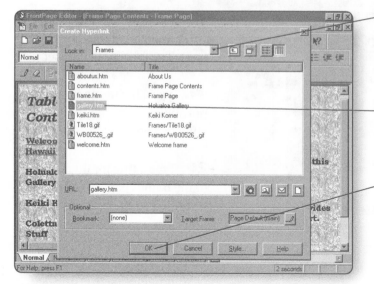

3. **Click** on the **folder** where the page to which you want to create the hyperlink is located. The folder will be selected.

4. **Click** on the **page** to which you want to create the link. The file will be selected.

5. **Click** on **OK**. The link to the page will be created.

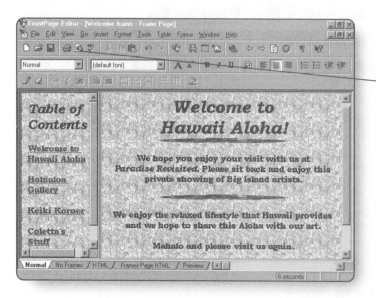

6. **Create hyperlinks** for each item in the contents frame.

7. **Click** on the **Preview in Browser button**. Your default Web browser will appear and you will be able to test your frames page.

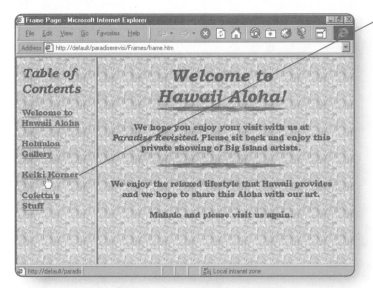

8. Click on a **hyperlink** in the navigation frame. The corresponding Web page will appear in the contents frame.

MAKING CHANGES TO THE FRAMES PAGE

After previewing your frames page, you may decide that you want to change the size or appearance of the individual frames in the frames page. Here are a few cosmetic enhancements that you can make to the frames page.

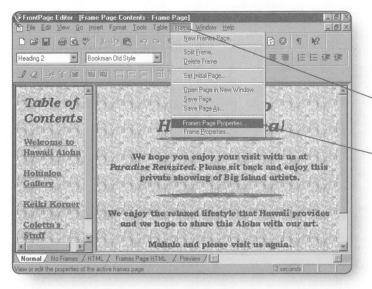

Changing Frame Spacing and Borders

1. Click on **Frame**. The Frame menu will appear.

2. Click on **Frames Page Properties**. The Page Properties dialog box will appear with the Frames tab displayed.

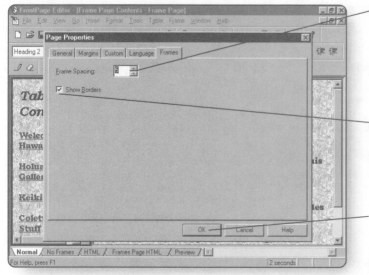

3. **Click** on the **up** and **down arrows** to the right of the Frame Spacing: text box to increase or decrease the pixels between the frame border areas.

4. **Click** on the **Show Borders check box** to hide the borders surrounding each frame that make up the frames page.

5. **Click** on **OK**. Your changes will be made.

NOTE

Frame borders make it easier for your visitors to understand how to navigate around your frames page.

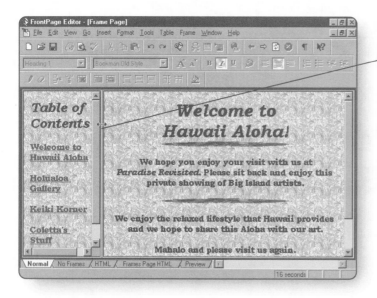

Resizing a Frame

1. **Click** and **hold** the **mouse button** on the border between the frames. The mouse pointer will change to a double arrow.

2. **Drag** the **mouse pointer** in either direction. The frames will change size.

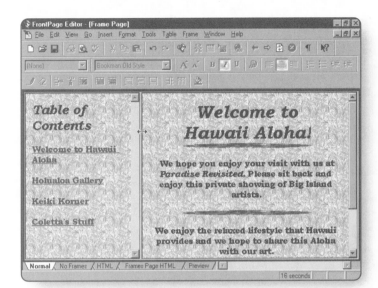

3. Release the **mouse button** when the frames are the desired size.

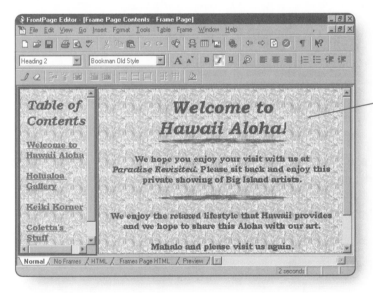

Controlling Scrollbars and Borders

1. Click in the **frame** that you want to set controls for scroll bars and borders. The frame will be selected.

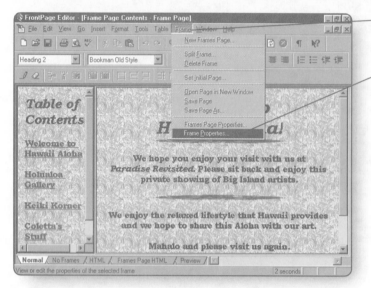

2. **Click** on **Frame**. The Frame menu will appear.

3. **Click** on **Frame Properties**. The Frame Properties dialog box will appear.

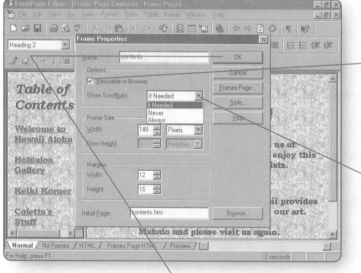

4. **Choose** from the following options:

✦ **Resizable in Browser.** This option gives your visitors the ability to change the size of the frames in their Web browser window.

✦ **Show Scrollbars.** This option sets how scroll bars should appear in your visitor's Web browser.

5. **Click** on **OK**. The control settings for the scroll bars and borders for the frame will be applied.

ADDING AND DELETING FRAMES

After your frames page has been created, it's still easy to add and delete frames.

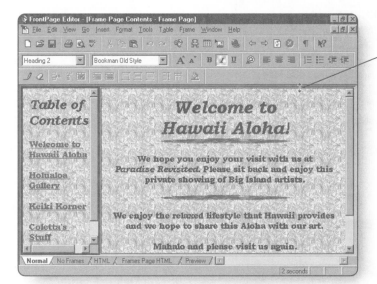

Adding Frames

1. **Place** the **mouse pointer** next to the frame border where you want to create the new frame. The mouse pointer will change to a double arrow.

2. **Press** and **hold** the **Ctrl key.**

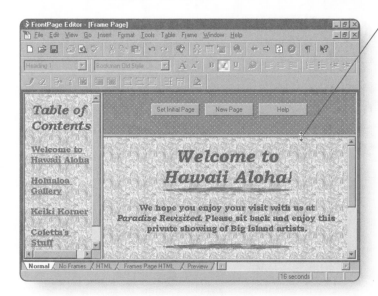

3. **Click** and **hold** the **mouse button** and **drag** the **mouse pointer** away from the area where you want the new frame created. A new frame will appear.

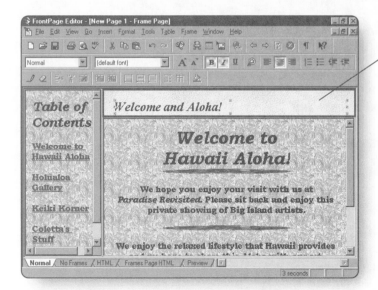

Deleting Frames

1. **Click** on the **frame** that you want to delete. The frame will be selected.

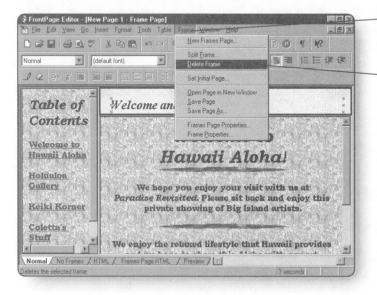

2. **Click** on **Frame**. The Frame menu will appear.

3. **Click** on **Delete Frame**. The frame will be deleted.

PART IV REVIEW QUESTIONS

1. What are the two methods for creating a hyperlink to a page on the Web? *See "Creating Links to Pages on the Web" in Chapter 11.*

2. How can you direct a visitor to a certain place on a Web page? *See "Creating Links to Bookmarks" in Chapter 11.*

3. Can the hyperlink colors used by a theme be changed? *See "Selecting Hyperlink Colors" in Chapter 11.*

4. How do you change the width of the outline that appears around hyperlinked images? *See "Adjusting the Image Border" in Chapter 12.*

5. How do you add messages to your Web pages? *See "Attaching Screen Messages to Images" in Chapter 12.*

6. What are the two border effects that you can use on thumbnails? *See "Attaching Screen Messages to Images" in Chapter 12.*

7. What are the different shapes that you can use to create hotspots on image maps? *See "Designing Image Maps" in Chapter 12.*

8. Does the Themes feature of FrontPage work when building a frames page? *See "Creating the Frames page" in Chapter 13.*

9. What is the easiest way to add a new frame to an existing frames page? *See "Adding and Deleting Frames" in Chapter 13.*

10. How do you add or delete a frame after you have built the frames page? *See "Adding and Deleting Frames" in Chapter 13.*

PART V
Finishing Your Web

.gif
.jpg
ey.gif
a.jpg
ntpag.gif
ish.jpg
respond.gif
shark.gif
sunset.gif

URL: images

HTML   Preview

14 Updating your Web

Hopefully, you've been having fun creating your Web site. Has your web grown from a few pages and only two levels to a dozen pages on three levels? Is there also a collection of images and other multimedia elements that have found their way onto the pages? Have you glanced at your filing system lately? Many tend to ignore the stacks of files that pile up on their computer—but this task doesn't have to be such a chore. FrontPage uses the same easy-to-use file management system found in other Windows programs. It also does some of your site management tasks for you. In this chapter, you'll learn how to:

✦ Keep all your hyperlinks in good working order

✦ Manage the files used in a web

✦ Create a to-do list to keep your web project organized

VERIFYING HYPERLINKS

During your Internet travels, you've probably clicked on a hyperlink that lead you nowhere. If you're a good netizen, you sent the Webmaster a message letting him know of the broken link. It's a big job for a Webmaster to keep an entire site current. Or maybe you just moved on. There is something you can do to make sure this doesn't happen at your Web site. The following sections will show you how to find and repair broken hyperlinks.

Checking All the Hyperlinks in a Web

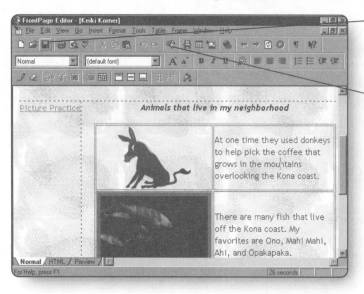

1. **Save** any **changes** that you may have made on all open pages.

2. **Click** on the **Show FrontPage Explorer button**. The FrontPage Explorer will appear.

NOTE

Before you can begin checking your hyperlinks, you will need to be connected to the Internet.

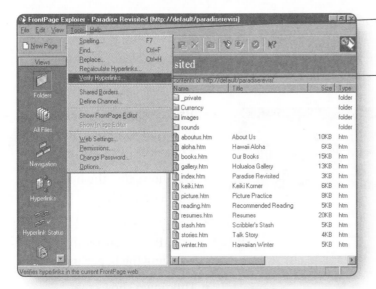

3. Click on **Tools**. The Tools menu will appear.

4. Click on **Verify Hyperlinks**. The Verify Hyperlinks dialog box will appear.

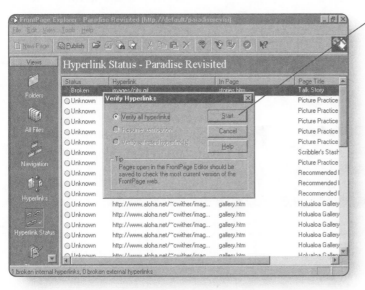

5. Click on the **Start button**.

FrontPage will begin verifying each hyperlink in the web. As FrontPage works down the list of hyperlinks, you can watch the validation progress. These symbols indicate the status of each hyperlink:

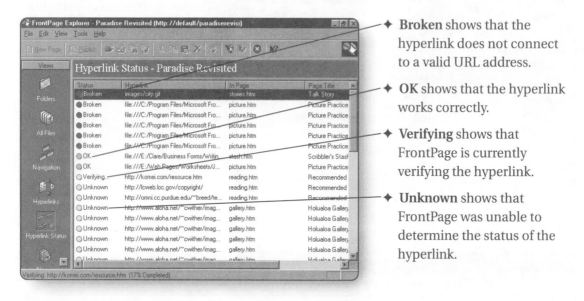

♦ **Broken** shows that the hyperlink does not connect to a valid URL address.

♦ **OK** shows that the hyperlink works correctly.

♦ **Verifying** shows that FrontPage is currently verifying the hyperlink.

♦ **Unknown** shows that FrontPage was unable to determine the status of the hyperlink.

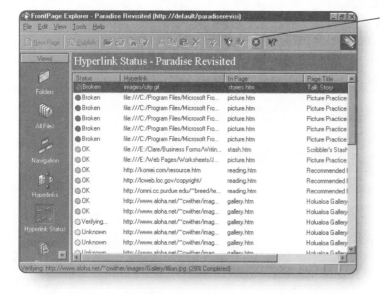

6. Click on the **Stop** button. FrontPage will stop verifying the status of hyperlinks.

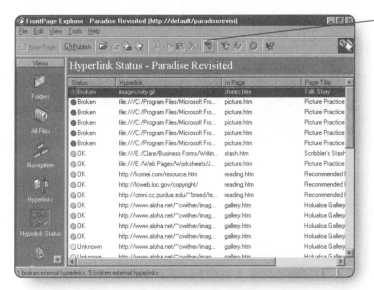

7. Click on the **Verify Hyperlinks button**. The Verify Hyperlinks dialog box will appear with the Resume verification option button selected.

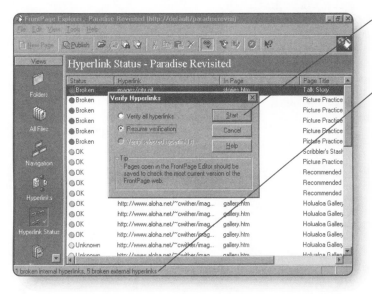

8. Click on the **Start button**. FrontPage will resume verifying the status of all the hyperlinks.

9. The Status bar lets you know how many external and internal hyperlinks are broken.

NOTE

When you close FrontPage, the program does not store the information collected about the hyperlink status.

Checking Selected Hyperlinks in a Web

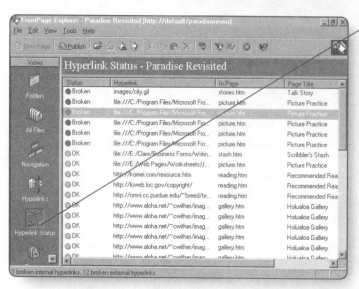

1. Click on the **Hyperlink Status view button.** A list of all hyperlinks contained in the web will appear in the right pane of the view window.

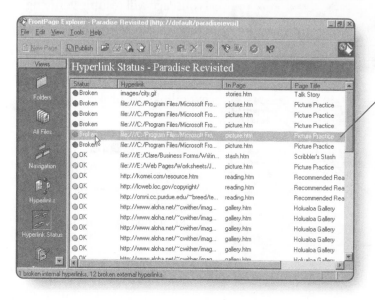

2. Select the **hyperlinks** you want verified using one of these methods:

✦ To select a single hyperlink, click on it.

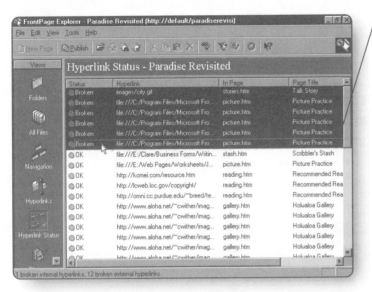

✦ To select a range of hyperlinks, click on the first hyperlink, press and hold the Shift key, then click on the last hyperlink.

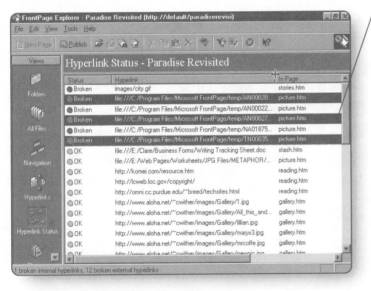

✦ To select random hyperlinks, click on the first hyperlink, press and hold the Ctrl key while clicking on each additional hyperlink.

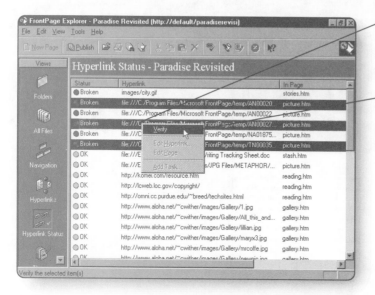

3. **Right-click** on any highlighted **hyperlink**. A menu will appear.

4. **Click** on **Verify**. FrontPage will verify the status of the hyperlinks and display the results in the Hyperlink Status window.

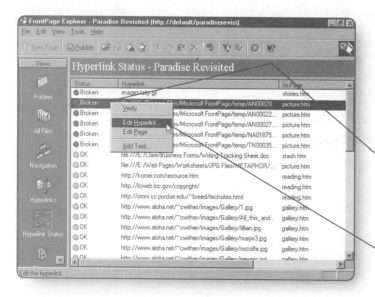

Fixing Hyperlinks

Any hyperlink that displays a broken status will need to be repaired.

1. **Right-click** on the broken internal **hyperlink** that you want to repair. A shortcut menu will appear.

2. **Click** on **Edit Hyperlink**. The Edit Hyperlink dialog box will appear.

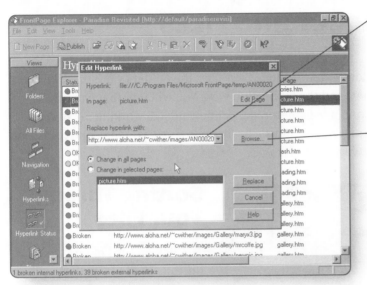

3. **Type** the correct **URL** for the hyperlink in the Replace hyperlink with: text box.

4. **Choose** one of the following **option buttons**:

✦ **Change in all pages**. To repair the broken hyperlink in every place that it appears in the web, click on this option button.

✦ **Change in selected pages**. To repair the broken hyperlink only on selected pages in the web, click on this option button and click on the pages where you want the hyperlink fixed.

5. **Click** on **Replace**. The status of the hyperlink will change.

MANAGING FILES

There are three different views in the FrontPage Explorer that allow you to manage your files: the Folders view, the All Files view, and the Navigation view. You will find that working in FrontPage Explorer feels somewhat like working in Windows Explorer. For routine file maintenance, you may find it easiest to work in Folders view.

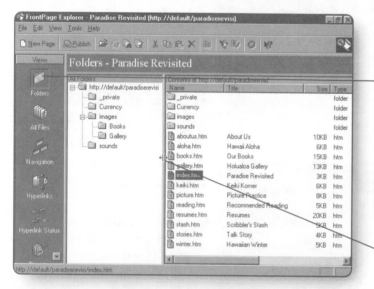

Sorting Through Your Files

1. Click on the **Folders view button**. The Folders View will appear in the FrontPage Editor window.

2. Change the **viewing area** using any of the following methods:

◆ Change frame size by placing the mouse pointer over the frame border, click and hold the mouse button, drag the frame border to the desired position, and release the mouse button.

◆ Change the column size by placing the mouse pointer between the two column headings, click and hold the mouse button, drag the column border to the desired position, and release the mouse button.

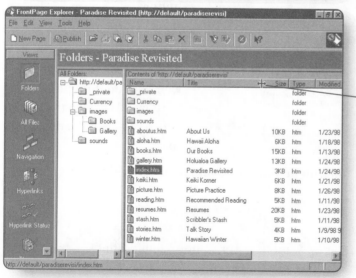

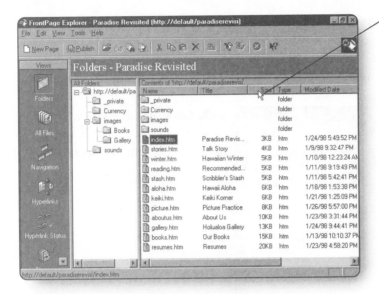

♦ Change the order of column entries by clicking on the column header of the column that you want to sort.

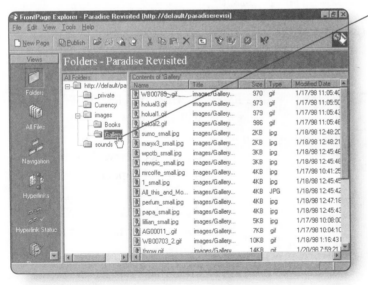

♦ View the contents of a folder by clicking on the folder.

Organizing Your Filing System

The easiest way to organize your web files is to create folders and move groups of files that belong together into these folders.

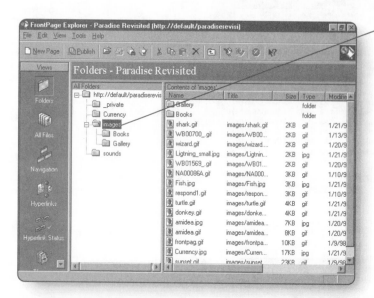

1. Click on the **folder** where you want the new folder to appear. The folder will be selected.

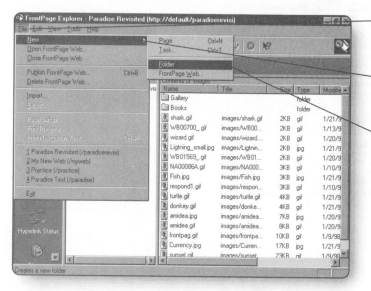

2. Click on **File**. The File menu will appear.

3. Click on **New**. A second menu will appear.

4. Click on **Folder**. A New Folder icon will appear in the Contents list.

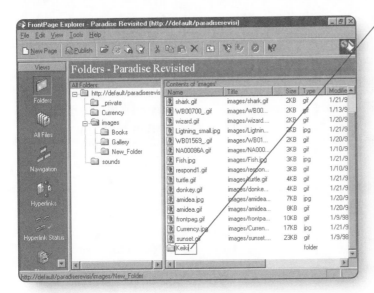

5. **Type** a **name** for the folder. The folder name will replace the "New Folder" text.

6. **Press Enter**. The new folder will be created. Now you can begin moving files to the new folder.

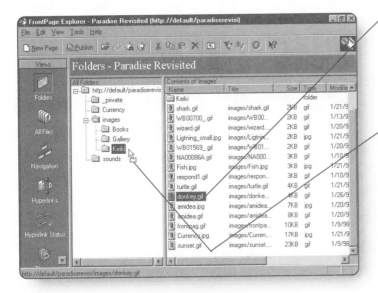

7. **Click** and **hold** on the **file** that you want to move. The file will be selected and the mouse pointer will have a gray box attached to it.

8. **Drag** the **mouse button** to the folder where you want to place the file and **release** the **mouse button**. The Rename dialog box will appear.

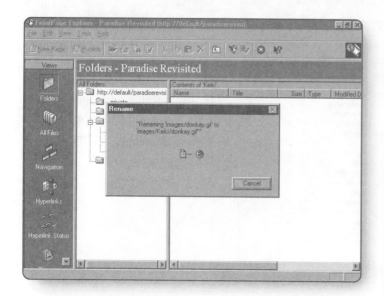

NOTE
FrontPage automatically changes any internal hyperlinks that are associated with the file that you just moved. You will not need to edit any hyperlinks and figure out which hyperlinks are associated with the moved file. When FrontPage has finished recalculating all the hyperlinks associated with the file, the file appears in its new folder.

Viewing File Attributes

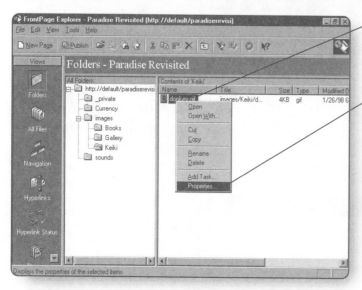

1. **Right-click** on the **file** whose attributes you want to view. A shortcut menu will appear.

2. **Click** on **Properties**. The Properties dialog box will appear with the General tab displayed.

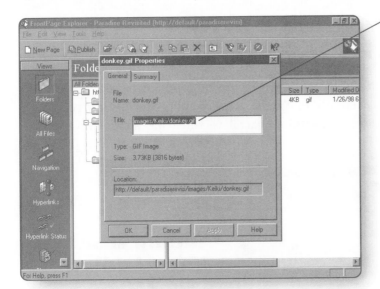

3. Type a new **title** for the file in the Title: text box, if needed.

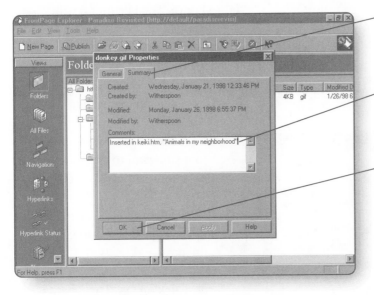

4. Click on the **Summary tab**. The Summary dialog box will appear.

5. Type any **comments** you want to save about the file in the Comments: text box.

6. Click on **OK**. The changes you make to the file's properties will be applied.

WORKING WITH THE TASKS LIST

While you have been working on your Web pages, you may have noticed that some of the FrontPage dialog boxes contain a button or an option that allows you to add a task. This feature of FrontPage creates a to-do list that will help you keep track of work that needs to be done. With this task list, you can assign a priority or delegate the task.

Adding Tasks When Adding a New Page

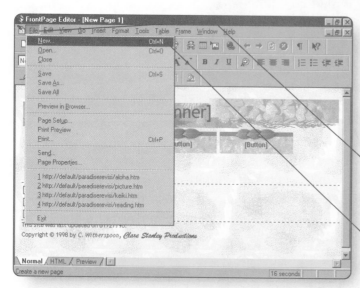

1. Click on **File** in the FrontPage Editor. The File menu will appear.

2. Click on **New**. The New Dialog box will appear with the Page tab displayed.

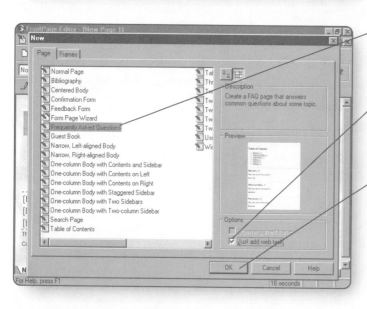

3. Click on the **type of page** that you want to create. The page template will be selected.

4. Click on **Just add web task**. A check mark will appear in the box.

5. Click on **OK**. The Save As dialog box will appear.

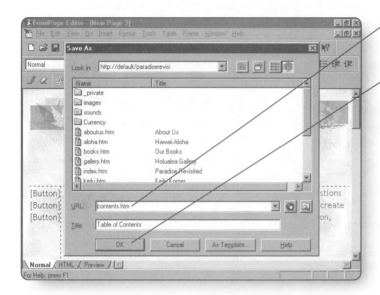

6. Type a **file name** and **title** for the Web page.

7. **Click** on **OK**. The new page will not appear in the FrontPage Editor window, but as a task in the Task List.

Adding Tasks During a Spell Check

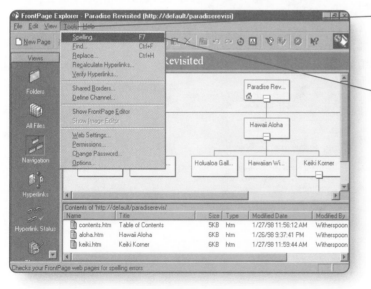

1. **Click** on **Tools** in the FrontPage Explorer. The Tools menu will appear.

2. **Click** on **Spelling**. The Spelling dialog box will appear.

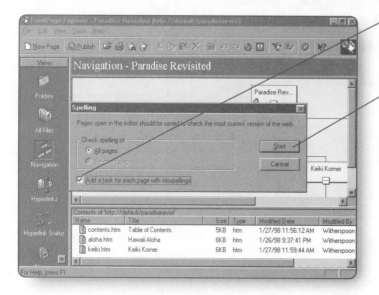

3. Click on **Add a task for each page with misspellings**. A check mark will appear in the box.

4. Click on **Start**. The spell check will check each page for misspelled words and add a task to the list for each page that contains misspellings.

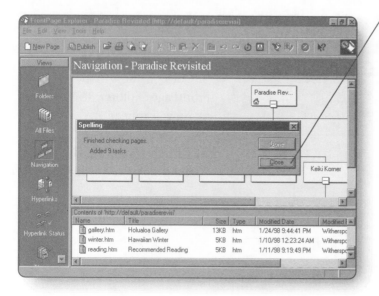

5. Click on the **Close button**. The tasks will be added to the Task List and will be waiting for you when you want to tackle this job.

Creating a New Task from the FrontPage Explorer

There may be times where you will want to add a task without first having to perform some action (such as creating a new page or spell checking). For example, you may want to remind yourself to do some research on a topic that you are covering in your web. You may want to make some changes to an image you added to a particular Web page. You can add these reminders to the Task List.

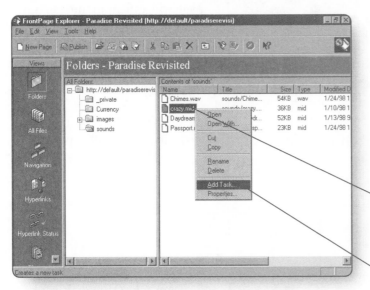

1. Right-click on the **file** to which you want to assign a task. A shortcut menu will appear.

2. Click on **Add Task**. The New Task dialog box will appear.

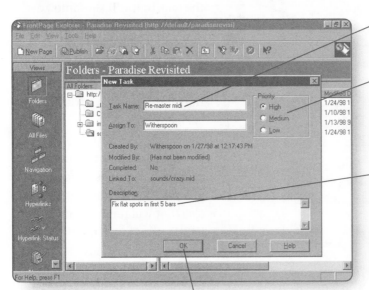

3. Type a descriptive **title** for the task in the Task Name: text box.

4. Click on an **option button** to select the priority to be given to the task. The option will be selected.

5. Type a **description** of the problem, the steps needed to be taken on the file, or anything else that will remind you how to handle the task in the Description: text box.

6. Click on **OK**. The new task will be added to the Tasks List.

Creating a New Task from the FrontPage Editor

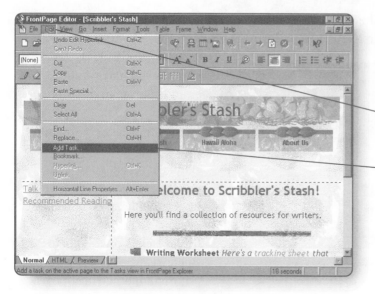

1. **Open** the **page** to which you want to assign the task. The page will appear in the FrontPage Editor.

2. **Click** on **Edit**. The Edit menu will appear.

3. **Click** on **Add Task**. The New Task dialog box will appear.

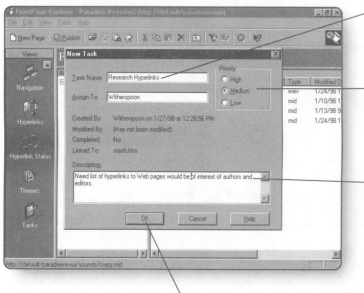

4. **Type** a descriptive **title** for the task in the Task Name: text box.

5. **Click** on an **option button** to select the priority to be given to the task. The option will be selected.

6. **Type** a **description** of the problem, the steps needed to be taken on the file, or anything else that will remind you how to handle the task in the Description: text box.

7. **Click** on **OK**. The new task will be added to the Tasks List.

Completing Tasks

Now that you've given yourself all this work to do, it's time to see what is listed and get some of it done.

1. **Click** on the **Tasks button**. The Tasks list will appear.

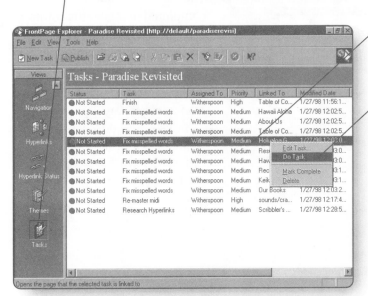

2. **Right-click** on the **task** on which you want to work. A shortcut menu will appear.

3. **Click** on **Do Task**. If you added a task to create a new page, the new page will appear in the FrontPage Editor window.

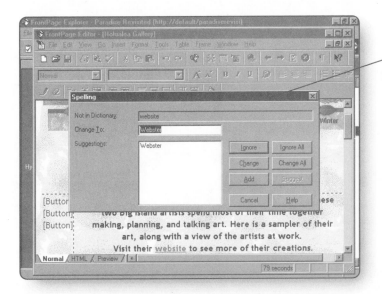

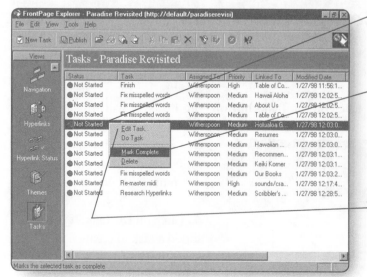

4. **Right-click** on the **task** that you just completed. A shortcut menu will appear.

5. **Click** on **Mark Complete**. The task will be shown as completed in the Status column.

TIP

If you want to make changes to any item in the Tasks List, right-click on the item and select Edit Task. The Task Details dialog box will appear and you can make the necessary changes.

15 Turning Your Web into a Channel

If you have enabled the Active Desktop of Internet Explorer 4.0, you've noticed the channel bar that appears on your screen. This channel bar contains icons for a number of channel providers. Just because there are some big names listed on the channel bar doesn't mean that you can't provide this same service to your visitors. Using FrontPage, channels are easy to create, and they are a great way for your regular visitors to keep current with what's happening at your web. Don't worry if your visitors aren't using Internet Explorer 4.0, because they can also subscribe to your channel if they're using Netscape Communicator 4.0. In this chapter, you'll learn how to:

✦ Build a channel file

✦ Preview your channel

✦ Update and make changes to your channel

CREATING THE CHANNEL FILE

As with most new technologies, building a channel and adding it to a Web site was once the domain of computer programmers and techno-nerds. Well, this is no longer the case. Microsoft has taken its Wizard technology and applied it to channels. Building a channel of your own is now a snap. Just follow the wizard.

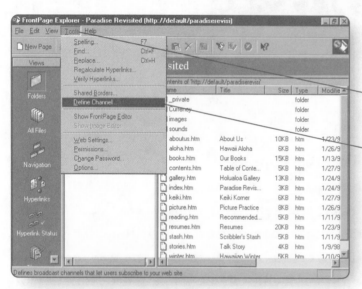

1. Open the **web** for which you want to create a channel in the FrontPage Explorer.

2. Click on **Tools**. The Tools menu will appear.

3. Click on **Define Channel**. The Channel Definition Wizard will start with the Welcome screen displayed.

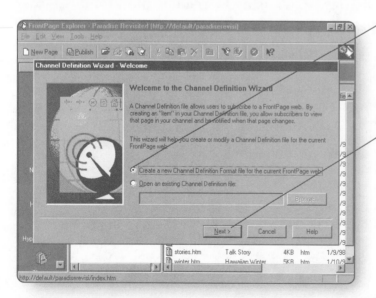

4. Click on the **Create a new Channel Definition Format file for the current FrontPage web option button**. The option will be selected.

5. Click on **Next**. The Channel Description screen of the wizard will appear.

6. Type a **title** for the channel in the Title: text box.

7. Type a **description** of the channel in the Abstract: text box. The abstract text will appear as a screen tip when your visitor holds the mouse pointer over the channel logo.

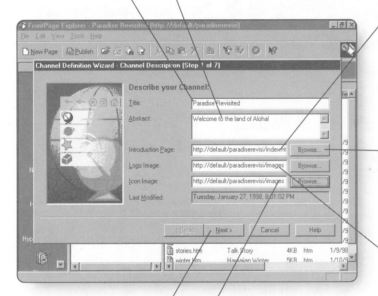

8. Type the **path** and **file name** for the page that you want to appear when a visitor subscribes to your channel.

TIP

If you don't know the path and file name of the page, click on the Browse button and search for the page.

9. Type the **path** and **file name** for the image that you want to use as your channel logo. This logo will identify the channel in the visitor's Web browser.

10. Type the **path** and **file name** for the image that you want to use as your page icons. This icon will identify the pages contained in the channel.

11. Click on **Next**. The Choose Source Folder screen of the wizard will appear.

NOTE

It is not required that you specify images for the channel logo and page icons. If you do use these images, both should be in GIF format. The logo image should be sized at 80×32 pixels and the page icon should be sized at 16×16 pixels.

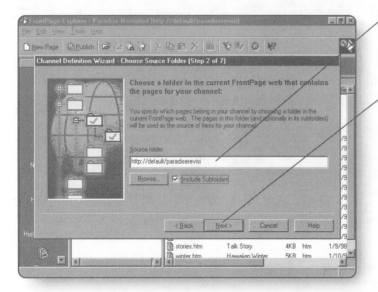

12. Type the **folder name** where the files are located that you want to use in the channel.

13. Click on **Next**. The Edit Page List screen of the wizard will appear.

NOTE

If you don't want the channel to contain your entire web, create a new folder in the FrontPage Explorer and place the files that you want contained in your channel in this folder. This isn't necessary, but it may make the next screen of the wizard easier.

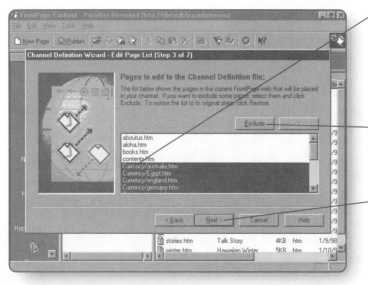

14. Press and **hold** the **Ctrl key** and **click** on those **files** that you do not want included in your channel. The files will be selected.

15. Click on the **Exclude button**. The selected files will be deleted from the list.

16. Click on **Next**. The Channel Item Properties screen of the wizard will appear.

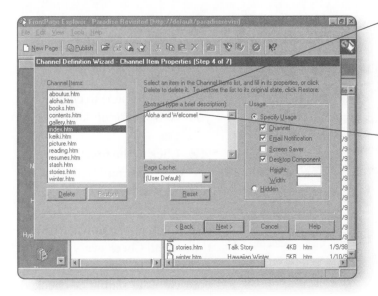

17. Click on the **page** in the Channel Items: list for which you want to change the properties. The page will be selected.

18. Type a **description** of the page in the Abstract (type a brief description): text box.

19. Choose from the following **Usage options**:

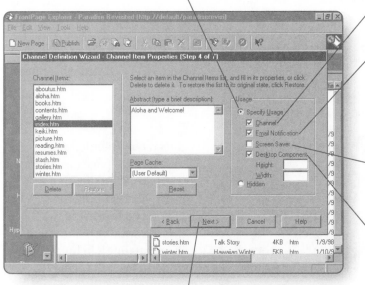

✦ **Channel** adds the selected page in the list of channel items.

✦ **E-mail Notification** sends a notice to those people who have subscribed to your channel when the channel is updated.

✦ **Screen Saver** allows the channel subscriber to use the page as a screen saver.

✦ **Desktop Component** displays a small window on the channel subscriber's desktop that contains information about the channel.

20. Click on **Next**. The Channel Scheduling screen of the wizard will appear.

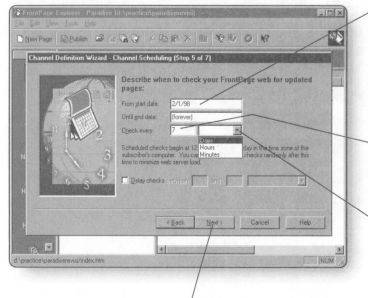

21. Double-click in the **From start date: text box** and **type** the **date** on which you want the channel (as installed on your visitor's computer) to check your Web site for updates.

22. Click in the first **Check every: text box** and **type** a **number**.

23. Click on the **down arrow** in the second Check every: text box and **select** the **interval** for when your Web site should be checked for updates.

24. Click on **Next**. The Log Target screen of the wizard will appear.

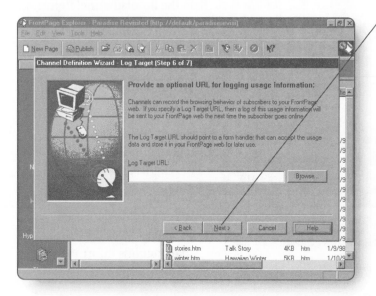

25. Click on **Next**. The Finish screen of the wizard will appear.

> **NOTE**
>
> It is recommended that novice Web page designers skip this step. Creating the form handler is an advanced topic. To find out more about form handlers, click on the Help button or refer to Prima's *Create FrontPage 98 Web Pages In a Weekend*.

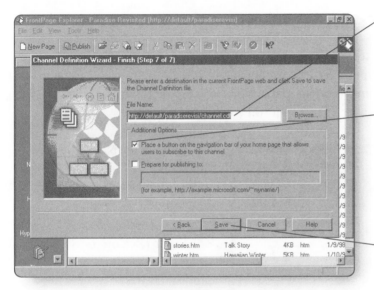

26. Use the **default location** for the channel definition format file displayed in the File Name: text box.

27. **Click** on the **Place a button on the navigation bar of your home page that allows users to subscribe to this channel check box**. A check mark will appear in the box.

28. **Click** on **Save**. The channel will be created and the channel definition file will appear in the list of files contained in your web.

NOTE

To make life a little simpler, you can wait to publish your channel when you publish the rest of your web. See Chapter 16, "Publishing Your Web."

Renaming the Channel Button

After your channel has been created, FrontPage adds a hyperlink to your main page entitled, "Subscribe." You may want your channel button to be more descriptive. Here's how to change the name on your channel button.

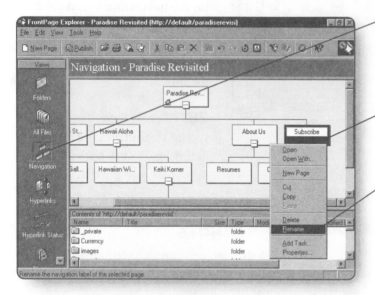

1. **Click** on the **Navigation button** in the Views bar. The navigation view will appear in the FrontPage Explorer.

2. **Right-click** on the **Subscribe page**. A shortcut menu will appear.

3. **Click** on **Rename**. The page title will be highlighted.

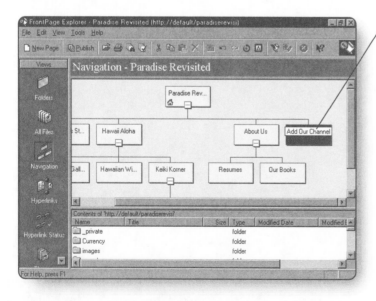

4. **Type** a **new name** for the Subscribe page and press the Enter key. The new title will appear on the page icon.

TESTING YOUR CHANNEL OFFLINE

Before you publish your channel, you will want to make sure that your channel works and looks the way you planned. It takes a few more steps to preview a channel than it does to preview a Web page, but it's still an easy process.

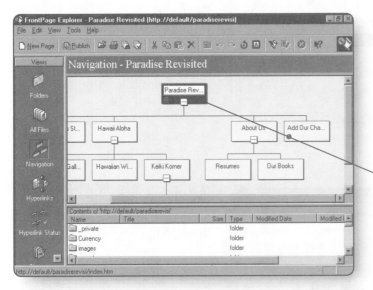

1. **Open** the **page** that contains the link to the channel definition file. The page will appear in the FrontPage Editor.

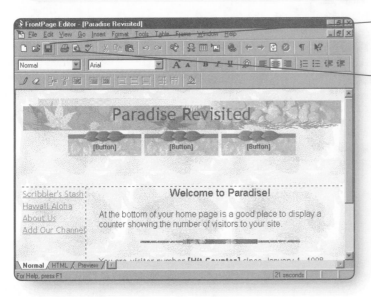

2. **Click** on the **Save button**. The page will be updated.

3. **Click** on the **Preview in Browser button**. Your default Web browser will open and the page will display.

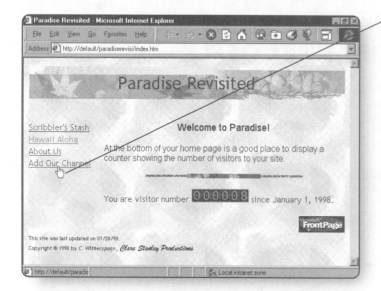

4. **Click** on the **channel hyperlink**. The Security Alert dialog box will appear, asking if you want to add the channel desktop component to your desktop.

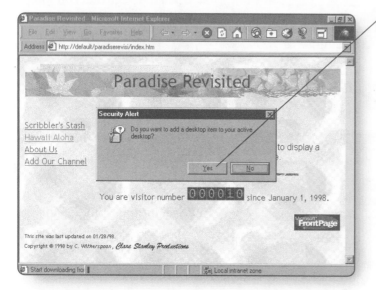

5. **Click** on **Yes**. The Add Active item to Active Desktop dialog box will appear.

6. **Click** on **OK**. The component will be added to your desktop.

NOTE

You will have to minimize all open programs to see the desktop component.

MAKING CHANGES TO YOUR CHANNEL

You've built a channel, previewed it, and now you want to make some changes. Making changes to your channel is as easy as building it.

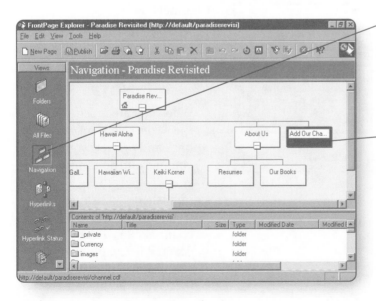

1. **Click** on the **Navigation view button** in the FrontPage Explorer. The Navigation view will appear in the FrontPage Explorer window.

2. **Double-click** on the **channel page**. The Channel Definition Wizard will appear.

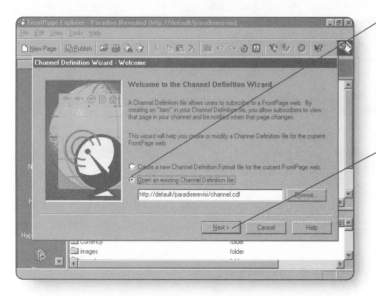

3. **Click** on the **Open an existing Channel Definition file option button**. The option will be selected and the path and file name for the channel will appear in the text box.

4. **Click** on **Next**. The next screen of the wizard will appear.

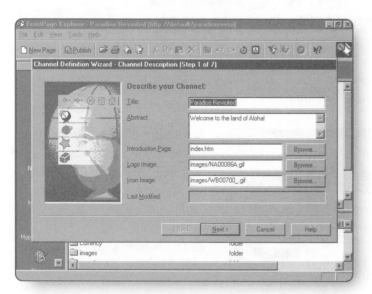

5. **Continue** through each **step** of the wizard and make your changes. For help with using the wizard, see the section in this chapter titled, "Creating the Channel File."

NOTE

When you are finished with the wizard, you can go back and preview your channel and determine if you are ready to be published. Publishing your web (and the included channel file) will be covered in Chapter 16, "Publishing Your Web."

16 Publishing Your Web

You've just spent days, or maybe weeks, building your web and making sure it works exactly the way you want. You've done a great job, so give yourself a pat on the back. You are now ready to publish your web so that the whole world can see your work. In this chapter, you'll learn how to:

✦ Find an ISP on whose server you can publish your web

✦ Use FrontPage to publish your web

✦ Use the Web Publishing Wizard to publish your web

DECIDING WHERE TO PUBLISH YOUR WEB

If you don't have an Internet Service Provider (ISP), or if your ISP doesn't provide space on its server to publish your web, you can use one of the ISP's (Microsoft calls them Web Presence Providers) that has made special arrangements with Microsoft to host webs for FrontPage users.

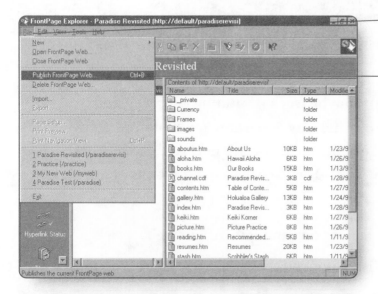

1. Click on **File**. The File menu will appear.

2. Click on **Publish FrontPage Web**. The Publish FrontPage Web dialog box will appear.

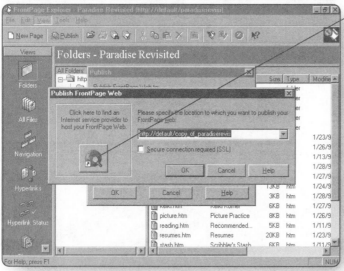

3. Click on the **Connect to the Microsoft FrontPage Web site button**. Your default Web browser will open and the Publish Your Site with a FrontPage WPP site will appear in the browser window.

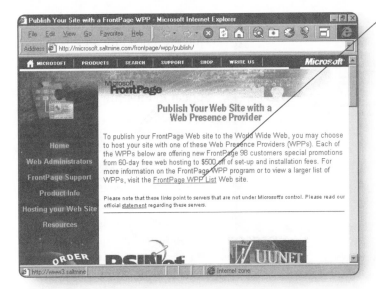

4. **Click** on the **FrontPage WPP list hyperlink**. The WPP List page will appear.

5. **Click** on the **down arrow** next to the View by State/Province search area. A list of states (shown by their two letter abbreviation) will appear.

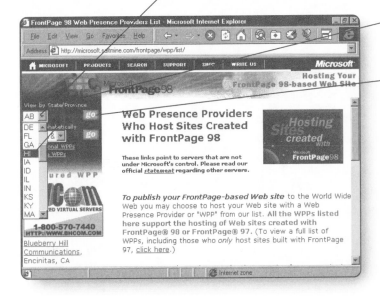

6. **Click** on your **state**. The state will be selected.

7. **Click** on the **Go hyperlink**. A list of Web Presence Providers in your state will appear in the browser window.

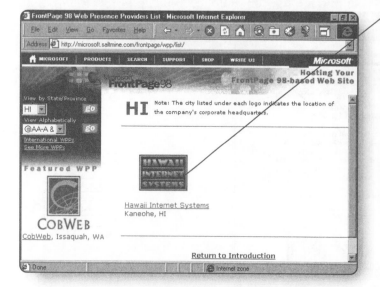

8. **Click** on the **hyperlink** for a Web Presence Provider. The FrontPage hosting page for the Web Presence Provider will appear in the browser window.

> ### NOTE
> Each of the Web Presence Providers lists its prices and services on its respective FrontPage hosting page. If you don't feel that this Web Presence Provider will suit your needs, click on your browser's Back button and look for another provider. You don't have to use a provider on the Microsoft list—you can choose your own.

GETTING ON THE WEB

There are two methods that you can use to publish your web to the Internet. The first method is the easiest: let FrontPage do it for you. This method only works if the Web server to which you are publishing supports the FrontPage Server Extensions. If your ISP does not support the FrontPage Server Extensions (you may have to call your ISP and ask its technical support personnel), you will have to use the Web Publishing Wizard.

Letting FrontPage Do It for You

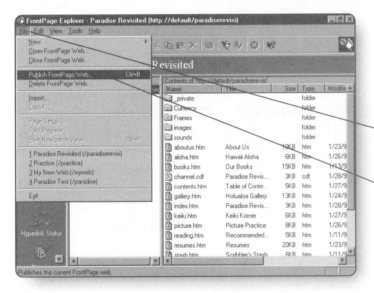

NOTE

Before you start publishing your web, make sure you are connected to your ISP.

1. **Click** on **File**. The File menu will appear.

2. **Click** on **Publish FrontPage Web**. The Publish FrontPage Web dialog box will appear.

NOTE

If the Publish FrontPage Web dialog box is still displayed on your screen after you search through the list of Web Presence Providers at the Microsoft Web site, you will need to skip steps 1 and 2.

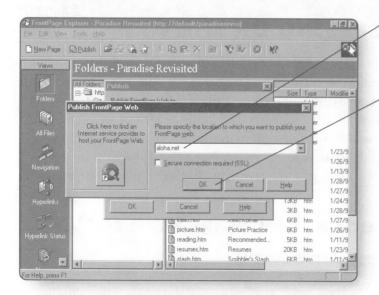

3. Type the **host name** of the provider to whose server you want to publish your web.

4. Click on **OK**.

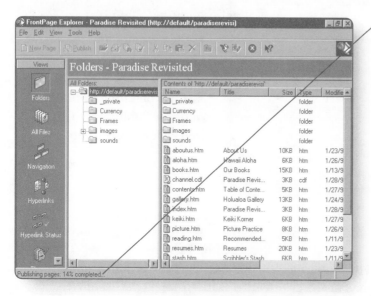

5. The status of the download will appear in the Status bar at the bottom of the FrontPage Explorer Window. When the download is complete, the Status bar will indicate that the web is published.

Using the Web Publishing Wizard

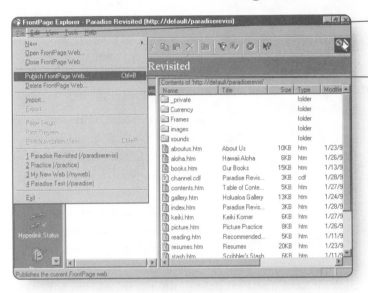

1. **Click** on **File**. The File menu will appear.

2. **Click** on **Publish FrontPage Web**. The Publish FrontPage Web dialog box will appear.

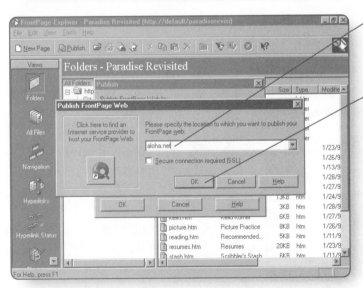

3. **Type** the **Host name** for the location to which you want to publish your web.

4. **Click** on **OK**. The Microsoft Web Publishing Wizard will appear.

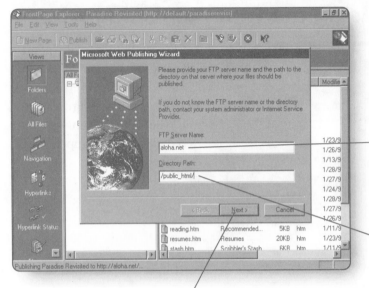

5. Type the **host name** for the location to which you want to publish your web in the FTP Server Name: text box.

6. Type the **directory** where your web is to be located in the Directory Path: text box.

7. Click on **Next**. The next page of the wizard will appear.

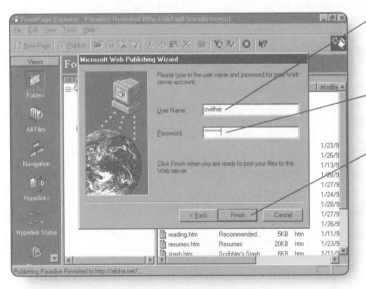

8. Type the **username** supplied to you by your ISP in the User Name: text box.

9. Type your **password** in the Password text box.

10. Click on **Finish**. The Transferring Files dialog box will appear and your web will begin downloading to your ISP's Web Server.

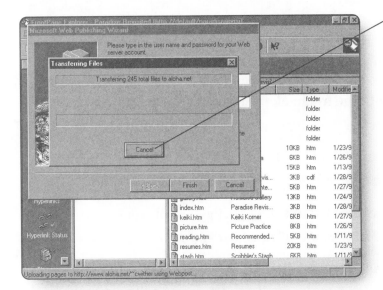

11. Click on **Cancel** if you wish to cancel the transfer.

PART V REVIEW QUESTIONS

1. How can you use FrontPage to check to see if the hyperlinks in your Web pages work correctly? *See "Verifying Hyperlinks" in Chapter 14.*

2. How do you sort a list of files in the FrontPage Explorer? *See "Sorting Through Your Files" in Chapter 14.*

3. How do you create a new folder in the FrontPage Explorer? *See "Organizing Your Filing System" in Chapter 14.*

4. How can you tell if a task can be added to the Task List so that you don't have to work on it right away and can be reminded to do it later? *See "Working with the Tasks List" in Chapter 14.*

5. In what two places can you create a new task? *See "Assigning New Tasks" in Chapter 14.*

6. What is the name of the wizard that helps you build a channel? *See "Creating the Channel File" in Chapter 15.*

7. How do you test a channel before you publish it? *See "Testing Your Channel Offline" in Chapter 15.*

8. How do you make changes to a channel that has already been created? *See "Making Changes to Your Channel" in Chapter 15.*

9. If you don't have any place to publish your web, where is one quick and easy place to find a possible ISP? *See "Deciding Where to Publish Your Web" in Chapter 16.*

10. What are the two different methods that FrontPage uses to publish your web to a Web server? *See "Getting on the Web" in Chapter 16.*

Appendix

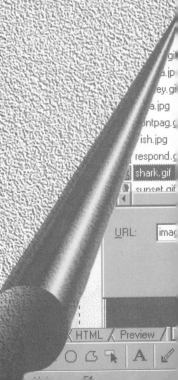

A
Creating a Custom Theme

In this book, you learned that the easiest way to give your web a professionally designed look is to use one of the themes that come with FrontPage. These themes are very attractive and cover a variety of tastes and needs. But what if you want to create your own banners, buttons, and bullets? Included on your FrontPage 98 CD-ROM is a nifty utility called Theme Designer. In this chapter, you'll learn how to:

✦ Add the Theme Designer to the FrontPage interface

✦ Access the Theme Designer

✦ Create your own custom theme

✦ Use your custom theme in a web.

INSTALLING THE THEME DESIGNER

The Theme Designer does not come preinstalled with FrontPage. It is one of the handy utilities that is included on the FrontPage CD-ROM. This section will show you where to find the Theme Designer and install it so that it becomes one of the FrontPage tools. First, close any programs that may be running on your computer and place the FrontPage CD-ROM into your CD-ROM drive.

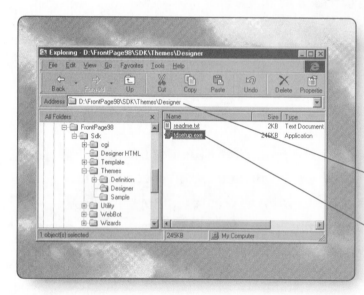

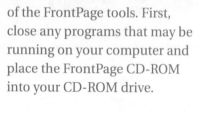

1. **Open Windows Explorer**. The Explorer window will appear.

2. **Open** the folder **\SDK\THEMES\DESIGNER**

3. **Double-click** on the file **tdsetup.exe**. The Microsoft FrontPage Theme Designer dialog box will appear.

4. **Click** on **Yes**. The Theme Designer will be installed on your computer and the Microsoft FrontPage Theme Designer dialog box will appear.

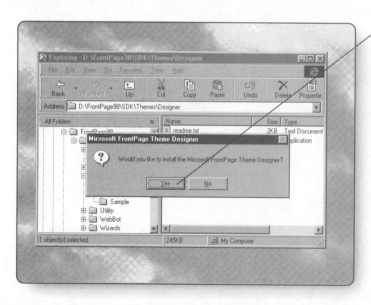

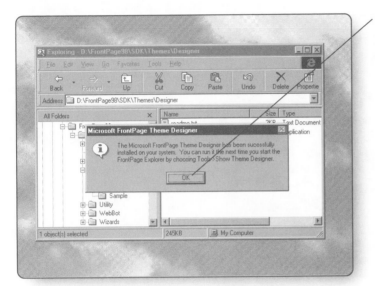

5. Click on **OK**. The Theme Designer can now be accessed from FrontPage.

OPENING THE THEME DESIGNER

Once you install the Theme Designer, it is easy to find within the FrontPage menus.

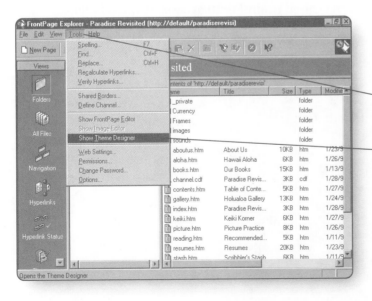

1. Open FrontPage. The FrontPage Explorer window will appear.

2. Click on **Tools**. The Tools menu will appear.

3. Click on **Show Theme Designer**. The Theme Designer window will appear.

The Theme Designer will appear on your screen with a blank window.

CREATING A NEW THEME

Now it's time for the fun to begin. If you haven't taxed your creative juices enough while building your web, you can stretch your creativity to the limit by creating your own theme that can be used in any FrontPage web that you build.

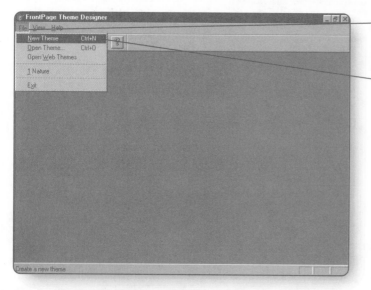

1. **Click** on **File**. The File menu will appear.

2. **Click** on **New Theme**. A theme template will appear in the Theme Designer Window.

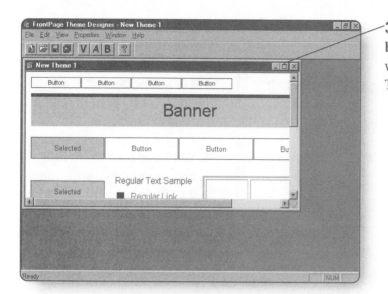

3. Click on the **Maximize button.** The theme template will appear full size in the Theme Designer window.

Applying a Solid Background

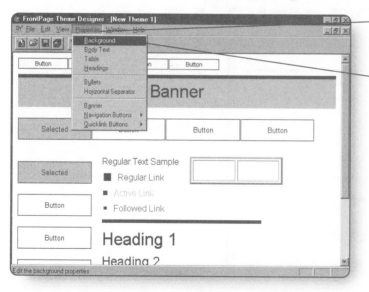

1. Click on **Properties**. The Properties menu will appear.

2. Click on **Background**. The Background Properties dialog box will appear with the Solid Background tab displayed.

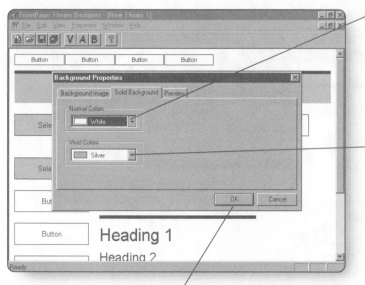

3. Click and hold the mouse button on the down arrow next to the Normal Colors list box and move the pointer to select the default background color for your web.

4. Click and hold the mouse button on the down arrow next to the Vivid Colors list box and move the pointer to select the background color that will be applied to a theme when the Vivid Colors option is selected.

5. Click on OK. The color that you chose as the Normal Color will appear as the background color for the theme.

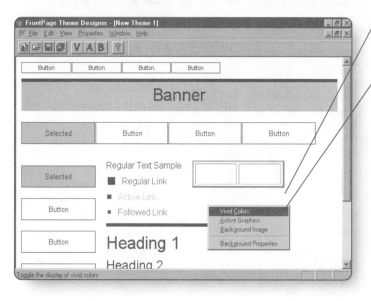

6. Right-click on the background. A shortcut menu will appear.

7. Click on Vivid Colors. The color that you chose as the Vivid Color will appear as the background color for the theme.

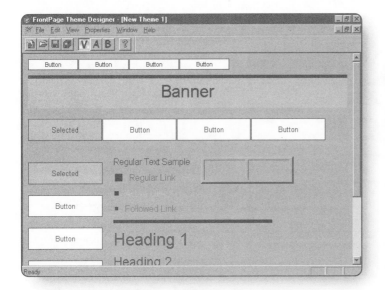

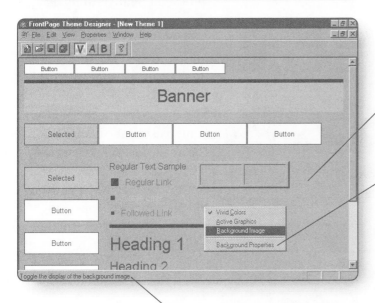

Using an Image in the Background

1. **Right-click** on the **background**. A shortcut menu will appear.

2. **Click** on **Background Properties**. The Background Properties dialog box will appear with the Solid Background tab displayed.

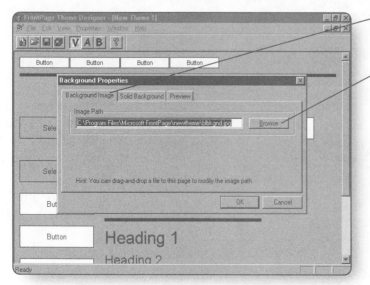

3. Click on the **Background Image tab**. It will come forward.

4. Click on the **Browse button**. The Open dialog box will appear.

TIP

There are several coordinated sets of banners, buttons, and images that you can download from the Microsoft Site Builder Network at: **http://www. microsoft.com/workshop/ design/creative/mmgallry. asp**

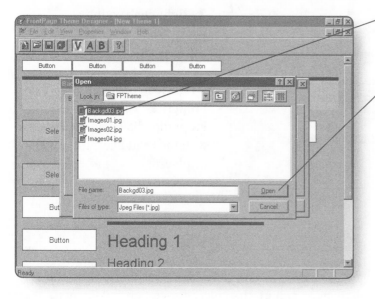

5. Click on the **file** that you want to use as the background. The image file will be selected.

6. Click on **Open**. The path and file name will appear in the Image Path text box of the Background Image tab.

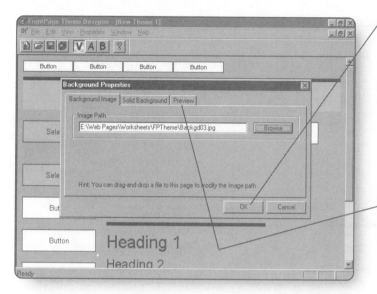

7. **Click** on **OK**. The default image for the theme will be applied.

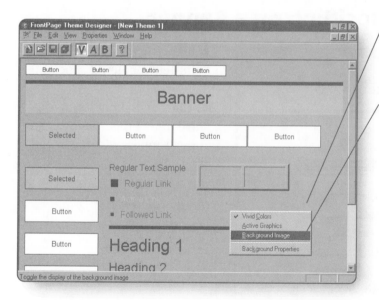

8. **Right-click** on the **background**. A shortcut menu will appear.

9. **Click** on **Background Image**. The background image you selected will appear in the theme window.

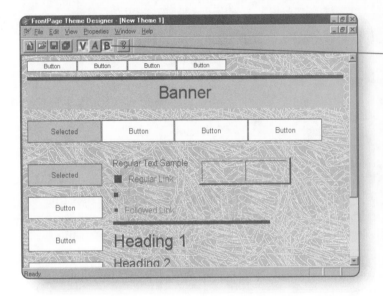

You now have three choices of backgrounds that you can use. You may want to alternate between backgrounds as you add banners, bullets, and buttons to see how different combinations of colors and images work together. You can use the V, A, and B buttons on the toolbar to toggle between these three backgrounds.

Deciding on a Banner

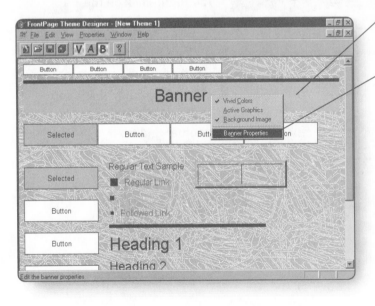

1. **Right-click** on the **Banner**. A shortcut menu will appear.

2. **Click** on **Banner Properties**. The Banner Properties dialog box will appear with the Image tab displayed.

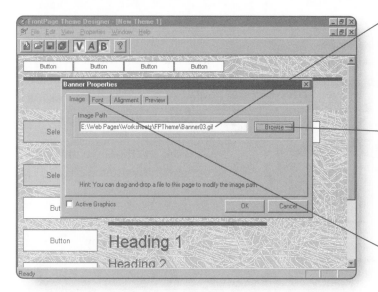

3. Type the **path and file name** of the image that you want to use as the theme banner.

NOTE

You can use the Browse button to locate the file on your computer and click on Open, as you did with the background.

4. **Click** on the **Font tab**. The Font properties will appear.

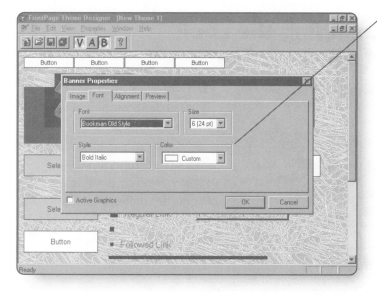

5. **Click** on the **Font**, font **Size**, font **Color**, and font **Style** that you want to appear on the banner. Your choices will be selected.

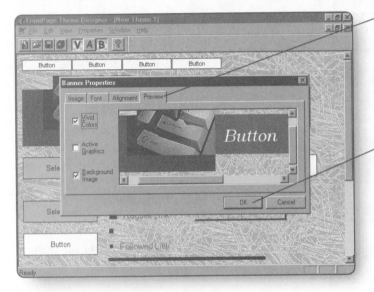

6. **Click** on the **Preview tab**. You will see what your banner will look like on the theme page. If you need to make any choices, click on the appropriate tab and make your changes.

7. **Click** on **OK**. The banner will appear on the theme page.

TIP

You won't find any help files if you look in the Help menu.

Changing the Look of the Body Text

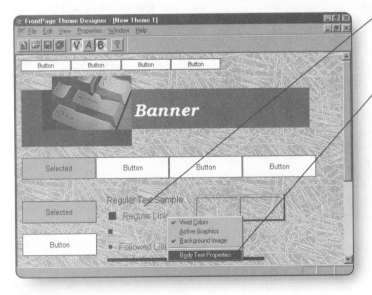

1. **Right-click** on any of the **Regular Text** samples. A shortcut menu will appear.

2. **Click** on **Body Text Properties**. The Body Text Properties dialog box will appear.

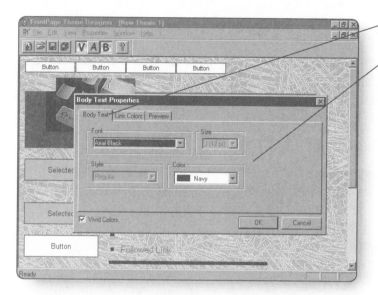

3. Click on the **Body Text tab**.

4. Click on the **Font** type and font **Color** that you want to use for the body text. Your choices will be selected.

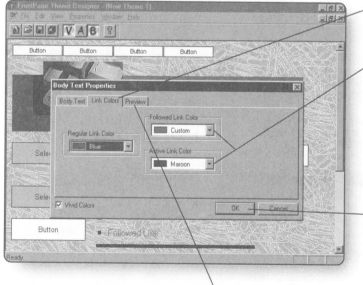

5. Click on the **Link Colors tab**. It will come forward.

6. Click on the **down arrow** next to the Regular Link Color, Followed Link Color, and Active Link Color drop-down lists and **click** on the **color** that you want to use for each of these hyperlink colors. The colors will be selected.

7. Click on **OK**. Your font style and hyperlink color choices will be applied to the theme.

> **NOTE**
>
> Use the Preview tab to see what your changes will look like before you apply your choices.

Sprucing Up Heading Styles

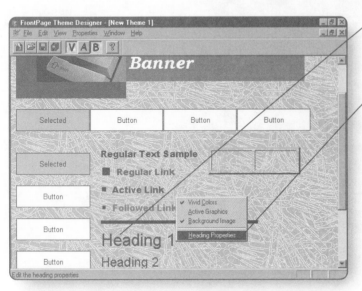

1. **Right-click** on the **Heading text**. A shortcut menu will appear.

2. **Click** on **Heading Properties**. The Heading Properties dialog box will appear with the tab of the Heading that you clicked on displayed.

NOTE

You can change all of the Heading styles from this one dialog box. Each Heading level has a corresponding tab section. Each of these tab sections works identically.

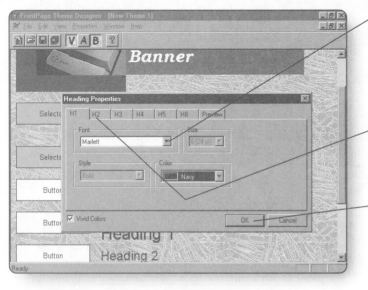

3. **Click** on the **down arrow** next to the Font and Color list boxes and **click** on the **Font Style** and **Font Color** that you want to use.

4. **Repeat step 3** for each heading level that you want to change.

5. **Click** on **OK**. The heading styles will be applied to your theme.

Making Your Point with Bullets and Rules

The bullets and the horizontal rule theme elements use almost identical dialog boxes to change the image used for the element.

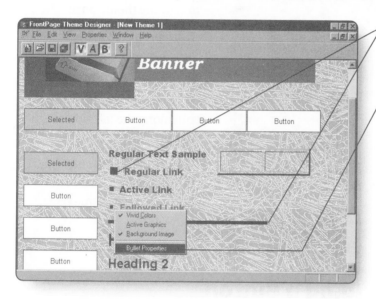

1. **Right-click** on a **Bullet** or the **Horizontal Rule**. A shortcut menu will appear.

2. **Click** on either **Bullet Properties** or **Horizontal Separator Properties**. The Properties dialog box for that theme element will appear.

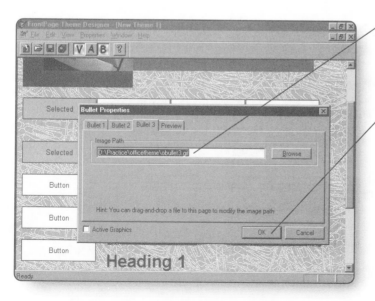

3. **Type** the **path** and **file name** for the image that you want to use for each theme element in the Image Path text box.

4. **Click** on **OK**. You will have some fancy looking images to set off your bullet points and separate blocks of text.

Creating Buttons

There are seven different buttons that you can apply images to in your theme:

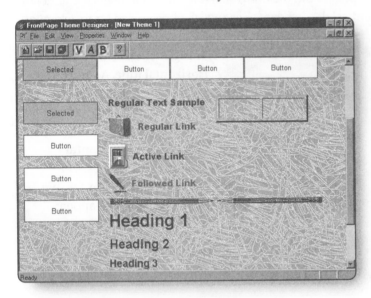

♦ **Global buttons** run along the top of the theme page

♦ **Horizontal Navigation buttons** are located under the banner

♦ **Vertical Navigation buttons** run along the left side of the theme window

♦ **Home**, **Up**, **Back**, and **Next buttons** are located at the bottom of the theme page.

Adding a Button

The method for adding each type of button is similar.

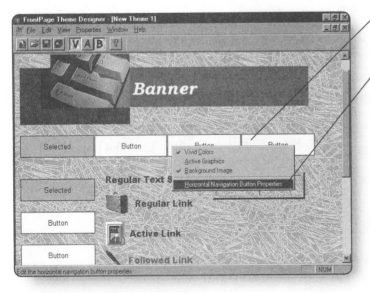

1. Right-click on a **button**. A shortcut menu will appear.

2. Click on **Button Properties** for the button type. The Button Properties dialog box will appear.

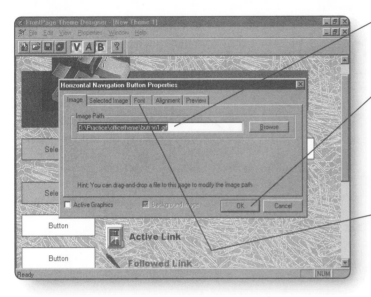

3. Type the **path** and **file name** of the image that you want to use for the button.

4. Click on **OK**. The button images will be applied to the theme.

NOTE

You can change the font and the font color that appears on the button by clicking on the Font tab in the Button Properties dialog box.

Coloring Your Tables

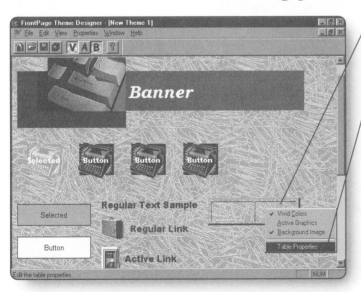

1. Right-click on the **table** theme element. A shortcut menu will appear.

2. Click on **Table Properties**. The Table Properties dialog box will appear.

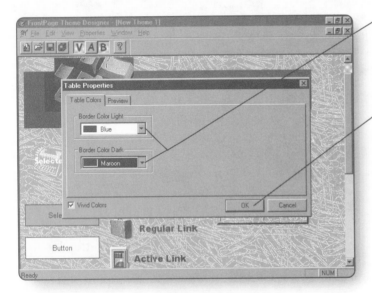

3. Click on the **down arrow** next to each of the list boxes and **select** the **colors** that you want for the table borders.

4. Click on **OK**. The table border colors will change in the theme page.

SAVING YOUR CUSTOM THEME

Before you can use your new theme in FrontPage, you will need to save the theme.

1. Click on the **Save button**. The Save As dialog box will appear.

2. Type a **title** for the theme in the Title text box.

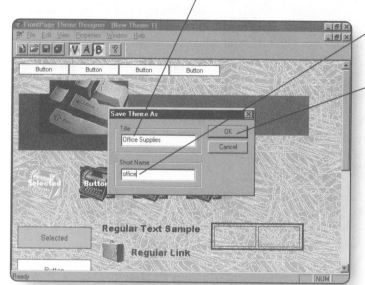

3. Type a **name** for the theme in the Short Name text box.

4. Click on **OK**. The theme will be saved along with the other themes that come with FrontPage.

NOTE

You can close the Theme Designer by clicking on the Close button.

USING YOUR CUSTOM THEME IN A FRONTPAGE WEB

Using your custom theme is as easy as using the themes that come preinstalled with FrontPage.

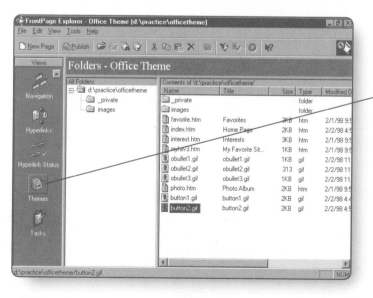

1. Open the **FrontPage Explorer**. The Explorer window will appear.

2. Click on the **Themes view**. The Themes window will appear.

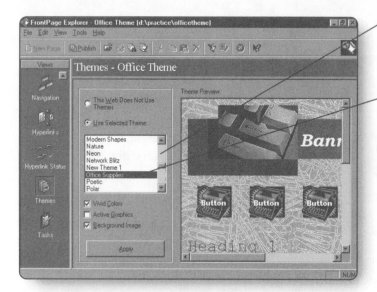

3. **Scroll** through the **list** of themes until you find the one you just created.

4. **Click** on your **custom theme**. A preview of the theme will appear. You can use your theme in any web you build.

Glossary

A

Active hyperlink. The currently selected hyperlink in a visitor's Web browser.

ActiveX control. A component of Dynamic HTML for adding features such as animation, video, credit card transactions, or financial calculation to Web pages.

All Files view. Shows all the files contained in the web and information about each one.

Animated GIF. A graphic file that contains several images. When these images are viewed in a Web browser, they act much like a short video (or cartoon).

Aspect ratio. The relationship between the height and width of an image.

B

Banner. A graphical image that usually appears at the top of a Web page and contains images, titles, or advertisements.

Banner Ad Manager. A dynamic HTML element used in FrontPage to display a series of images in a slideshow fashion with transitions between the images, if desired.

Bevel. An effect applied to images to give it the appearance of being inside a frame, much like a framed picture on an office wall.

Bookmark. A specific place on a page to which you can point with a hyperlink. When visitors click on a hyperlink to a bookmark, their Web browser will take them to that particular place on the page, not just the top of the page.

Broken hyperlink. A hyperlink that does not connect to another Web page.

Bullet list. A method of displaying an unordered list of items, with each item being set off by a bullet character.

C

Cell. Where a row and a column intersect in a table.

Cell padding. The space between the cell border and the contents of the cell.

Cell spacing. The width of the cell borders, measured in pixels.

Channel. A method that allows visitors to subscribe to a site so that they can view Web pages offline and be informed of when the site is updated.

Channel Definition Format. The type of file that makes it possible for visitors to view Web pages as a channel.

Clip art. Images, sounds, video, and other graphics that can be included in Web pages free of charge and without restriction.

Column. The vertical row of cells in a table.

Crop. To resize an image by deleting the outside edges. In FrontPage, this only occurs in a rectangular shape.

D

Desktop component. A small window that appears on a visitor's desktop when he chooses to subscribe to a Web site through a channel. It displays the channel on his desktop so that he can view the channel when he is offline.

E

Embedded files. Any images, sounds, or video files that are contained in Web pages.

External hyperlink. A link to a page that is not located in a personal web.

F

Files pane. A window in the FrontPage Explorer that displays the contents of a web. The Files pane looks much like the list of files in Windows Explorer.

Folders view. Displays how the web content is organized.

Form. A page that contains data fields that visitors to a Web site can fill in and then reply to either as an e-mail or as a file contained in the web on the Web server.

Form field. A data entry field on a form page.

Format toolbar. A toolbar in the FrontPage Editor for adding styles (such as bold or centering) to text and paragraphs.

Forms toolbar. A toolbar in the FrontPage Editor for adding form fields to a forms page.

Frame. One of a number of separate windows that appears in the browser window. These separate windows are usually separated by a border and can contain scroll bars.

Frames page. The Web page that controls how the individual frames appear when viewed in a Web browser.

FrontPage Editor. A tool for creating, designing, and editing Web pages to add text, images, tables, and forms. They will be displayed as they appear in a Web browser. The FrontPage Editor creates all the HTML code for you.

FrontPage Explorer. A tool for creating and managing a web.

FrontPage Server Extensions. Software programs that are stored on a Web server that support some of the advanced features of FrontPage and allow these features to work correctly.

G

GIF. Graphics Interchange Format. A file format used for image files that is commonly found on the Web. GIF files are usually comprised of drawings created in a computer graphics program and contain less than 256 colors. GIF files are highly compressed so that they transmit quickly over the Internet.

H

Heading. A type of paragraph style used to emphasize titles and introductions in Web pages. There are six different heading styles supported in FrontPage.

Home page. The first page that appears by default in a Web browser when accessing a Web site. The home page is usually named "index.htm" or "default.htm."

Horizontal rule. A line image that is used to separate sections of text in Web pages.

Hotspot. An area on an image map on which a visitor can click and be taken to another area of the web. An image map usually contains more than one hotspot.

Hover button. A navigational button on a Web page that becomes animated by either changing its color or image when the mouse pointer is placed over it.

HTML. Stands for Hypertext Markup Language. This is the programming language that is used to create Web pages. FrontPage creates all the HTML code automatically.

Hyperlink. The method used to move from Web page to Web page. A hyperlink can be linked to a word, a group of words, an image, or an image map. When a visitor clicks on one of the linked elements, the page that is linked to the hyperlink will appear in his Web browser.

Hyperlink Status view. Shows whether or not the hyperlinks contained in the web are linked to a valid page.

Hyperlinks view. Displays links between pages inside the web and links to pages outside the web.

I

Image. A picture or graphics file that is included in a Web page. Most images are in the GIF or JPEG format.

Image bullet. A picture or graphic that is used instead of the standard dot used in bulleted lists.

Image map. A picture or graphic that contains several hotspots on which visitors can click to be taken to different parts of a web.

Image toolbar. A toolbar that can be displayed in the FrontPage Editor that contains buttons to change the way images appear on the Web page.

Initial page. The first page that displays in a frame window when the frames page appears in the browser window.

Internal hyperlink. A link to a page, or a certain spot on a page, that is found within a web.

Internet. A global network of computers that provides public communication services to individuals, businesses, and organizations. Services provided by the Internet include e-mail, ftp, and Web browsing. The Web is only one part of the Internet.

Internet Explorer. The Web browser developed by Microsoft Corporation.

J

Java. A programming language created by Sun Microsystems. Java is used to create small programs that can be run from within a Web browser.

Java applet. A small program created using the Java programming language. Java applets are downloaded to a computer from a Web site. The computer executes the program, which runs in a Web browser.

JPEG. Stands for Joint Photographic Experts Group. A file format used on the Internet to display photographic quality images. JPEG files are compressed so that they can be downloaded quickly to display in Web pages.

M

Mailto. A type of hyperlink that allows visitors to a Web site to send an e-mail message. When the visitor clicks on the mailto hyperlink, a new message window displays from his default e-mail program.

Marquee. An area on a Web page that displays text that scrolls across the page.

N

Navigation buttons. Graphical elements in a Web page that help direct visitors to the different pages in a web.

Navigation view. Shows an organization chart of the web.

Nested list. A list that is a subset of the main list. Nested lists are normally indented from the mail list.

O

One-line text box. A form element that allows visitors to type short amounts of information into a form.

Option button. A form element that a visitor clicks on to indicate his selection.

P

Page. A single document within a web that contains text, graphics, hyperlinks, and other elements.

Page template. A predesigned page that can be used as a basis to create other pages. Templates contain standardized text, image placeholders, prebuilt tables, or any other elements.

Page title. The name of a particular Web page. The page title appears in any banners and also in the title bar of the Web browser used by visitors to a site.

Publish. To put a web on the Internet with a Web Service Provider.

R

Resample. To change the size of a graphic image.

Row. A horizontal collection of cells in a table.

S

Scrolling text box. A form element that allows visitors to input large amounts of text in a form. The text box takes up a specified area in the form but does not limit the amount of information that can be input. A visitor can view his input by using the scroll bars.

Shared borders. An area that can be set up on several Web pages so that any content input into these shared areas will appear in all pages.

Size handle. Small black boxes at the corners and sides of an image used to resize an image.

Standard toolbar. A toolbar found in the FrontPage Editor that contains buttons that execute menu commands.

Status bar. An area at the bottom of the FrontPage Explorer and FrontPage Editor that displays information about the current task or command.

Style. Shortcuts for adding formatting to text. Styles also help keep the text uniform.

T

Table. A collection of cells arranged in rows and columns. Tables are used to display information in a neat and organized manner. They can also be used as page layout elements to help keep text and graphics on a page.

Table toolbar. A toolbar found in the FrontPage Editor that makes it quick and easy to create, edit, and format tables.

Target frame. A frame in a frames page that displays the page linked to a hyperlink.

Task. An item that is placed in the FrontPage Task list. Also known as a to-do item.

Tasks view. Shows the parts of the web that are finished and unfinished.

Theme. A predesigned set of backgrounds, colors, images, navigation buttons, banners, and bullets. Themes are used to give a web a professional look. They also make it easy to get a web started.

Themes view. Allows you to choose a set of coordinated backgrounds and buttons for the web.

Thumbnail. A thumbnail image is a small version of an image on a page that contains a hyperlink to a full size version of the same image.

Transition effect. An effect that occurs, such as fade to black, when a Web page is accessed or exited.

u

URL. Stands for Uniform Resource Locator. The URL provides the Internet address for a Web site.

V

Visited hyperlink. A hyperlink on a Web page that has already been accessed by the Web browser.

W

Washout. An effect applied to graphic images to give them a faded or sun bleached look.

Web. A collection of Web pages that are linked together and are stored either on a computer or have been published on a Web server.

Index

YOUR COMMENTS
Send Us

Dear Reader:

Thank you for buying this book. In order to offer you more quality books on the topics *you* would like to see, we need your input. At Prima Publishing, we pride ourselves on timely responsiveness to our readers needs. If you'll complete and return this brief questionnaire, *we will listen!*

Name: (first) _____ (M.I.) _____ (last) _____

Company: _____ Type of business: _____

Address: _____ City: _____ State: _____ Zip: _____

Phone: _____ Fax: _____ E-mail address: _____

May we contact you for research purposes? ❏ Yes ❏ No

(If you participate in a research project, we will supply you with your choice of a book from Prima CPD)

❶ How would you rate this book, overall?

❏ Excellent   ❏ Fair
❏ Very Good   ❏ Below Average
❏ Good   ❏ Poor

❷ Why did you buy this book?

❏ Price of book   ❏ Content
❏ Author's reputation ❏ Prima's reputation
❏ CD-ROM/disk included with book
❏ Information highlighted on cover
❏ Other (Please specify): _____

❸ How did you discover this book?

❏ Found it on bookstore shelf
❏ Saw it in Prima Publishing catalog
❏ Recommended by store personnel
❏ Recommended by friend or colleague
❏ Saw an advertisement in: _____
❏ Read book review in: _____
❏ Saw it on Web site: _____
❏ Other (Please specify): _____

❹ Where did you buy this book?

❏ Bookstore (name)_____
❏ Computer Store (name) _____
❏ Electronics Store (name) _____
❏ Wholesale Club (name) _____
❏ Mail Order (name) _____
❏ Direct from Prima Publishing
❏ Other (please specify): _____

❺ Which computer periodicals do you read regularly? _____
_____
_____
_____

❻ Would you like to see your name in print?

May we use your name and quote you in future Prima Publishing books or promotional materials?

❏ Yes   ❏ No

❼ Comments & Suggestions: _____
_____
_____

8 Where do you use your computer?

Work	☐ 100%	☐ 75%	☐ 50%	☐ 25%
Home	☐ 100%	☐ 75%	☐ 50%	☐ 25%
School	☐ 100%	☐ 75%	☐ 50%	☐ 25%

Other _____

9 How do you rate your level of computer skills?

☐ Beginner
☐ Advanced
☐ Intermediate

10 What is your age?

☐ Under 18
☐ 18-24 ☐ 40-49
☐ 25-29 ☐ 50-59
☐ 30-39 ☐ 60-over

11 I would be interested in computer books on these topics

☐ Word Processing ☐ Database:
☐ Networking ☐ Spreadsheets
☐ Desktop Publishing ☐ Web site design

Other _____

PLEASE
PLACE
STAMP
HERE

PRIMA PUBLISHING

Computers & Technology
3875 Atherton Road
Rocklin, CA 95765

OTHER BOOKS FROM PRIMA PUBLISHING
Computers & Technology

ISBN	Title	Price
0-7615-1363-9	Access 97 Fast & Easy	$16.99
0-7615-1175-X	ACT! 3.0 Fast & Easy	$16.99
0-7615-1348-5	Create FrontPage 98 Web Pages In a Weekend	$24.99
0-7615-1294-2	Create PowerPoint Presentations In a Weekend	$19.99
0-7615-0692-6	Create Your First Web Page In a Weekend	$24.99
0-7615-0428-1	The Essential Excel 97 Book	$27.99
0-7615-0733-7	The Essential Netscape Communicator Book	$24.99
0-7615-0969-0	The Essential Office 97 Book	$27.99
0-7615-0695-0	The Essential Photoshop Book	$35.00
0-7615-1182-2	The Essential PowerPoint 97 Book	$24.99
0-7615-1136-9	The Essential Publisher 97 Book	$24.99
0-7615-0752-3	The Essential Windows NT 4 Book	$27.99
0-7615-0427-3	The Essential Word 97 Book	$27.99
0-7615-0425-7	The Essential WordPerfect 8 Book	$24.99
0-7615-1008-7	Excel 97 Fast & Easy	$16.99
0-7615-1194-6	Increase Your Web Traffic In a Weekend	$19.99
0-7615-1191-1	Internet Explorer 4.0 Fast & Easy	$19.99
0-7615-1137-7	Jazz Up Your Web Site In a Weekend	$24.99
0-7615-1379-5	Learn Access 97 In a Weekend	$19.99
0-7615-1293-4	Learn HTML In a Weekend	$24.99
0-7615-1295-0	Learn the Internet In a Weekend	$19.99
0-7615-1217-9	Learn Publisher 97 In a Weekend	$19.99
0-7615-1251-9	Learn Word 97 In a Weekend	$19.99
0-7615-1193-8	Lotus 1-2-3 97 Fast & Easy	$16.99
0-7615-1420-1	Managing with Microsoft Project 98	$29.99
0-7615-1382-5	Netscape Navigator 4.0 Fast & Easy	$16.99
0-7615-1162-8	Office 97 Fast & Easy	$16.99
0-7615-1186-5	Organize Your Finances with Quicken Deluxe 98 In a Weekend	$19.99
0-7615-1513-5	Publisher 98 Fast & Easy	$19.99
0-7615-1192-X	SmartSuite 97 Fast & Easy	$16.99
0-7615-1138-5	Upgrade Your PC In a Weekend	$19.99
1-55958-738-5	Windows 95 Fast & Easy	$19.95
0-7615-1007-9	Word 97 Fast & Easy	$16.99
0-7615-1316-7	Word 97 for Law Firms	$29.99
0-7615-1083-4	WordPerfect 8 Fast & Easy	$16.99
0-7615-1188-1	WordPerfect Suite 8 Fast & Easy	$16.99

To Order Books

Please send me the following items:

Quantity	Title	Unit Price	Total
_____	_____	$ _____	$ _____
_____	_____	$ _____	$ _____
_____	_____	$ _____	$ _____
_____	_____	$ _____	$ _____
_____	_____	$ _____	$ _____

Subtotal	$ _____
Deduct 10% when ordering 3-5 books	$ _____
7.25% Sales Tax (CA only)	$ _____
8.25% Sales Tax (TN only)	$ _____
5.0% Sales Tax (MD and IN only)	$ _____
7.0% G.S.T. Tax (Canada only)	$ _____
Shipping and Handling*	$ _____
Total Order	$ _____

*Shipping and Handling depend on Subtotal.

Subtotal	Shipping/Handling
$0.00–$14.99	$3.00
$15.00–$29.99	$4.00
$30.00–$49.99	$6.00
$50.00–$99.99	$10.00
$100.00–$199.99	$13.50
$200.00+	Call for Quote

Foreign and all Priority Request orders:
Call Order Entry department
for price quote at 916-632-4400
This chart represents the total retail price of books only
(before applicable discounts are taken).

By Telephone: With MC or Visa, call 800-632-8676 or 916-632-4400. Mon–Fri, 8:30-4:30.

WWW: http://www.primapublishing.com

By Internet E-mail: sales@primapub.com

By Mail: Just fill out the information below and send with your remittance to:

Prima Publishing
P.O. Box 1260BK
Rocklin, CA 95677

My name is _____

I live at _____

City_____ State_____ ZIP _____

MC/Visa#_____ Exp._____

Check/money order enclosed for $ _____ Payable to Prima Publishing

Daytime telephone _____

Signature _____

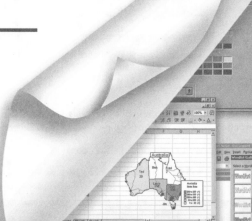